Barry or Jones

"Father of the United States Navy"

President Washington Personally Confers Commission No. 1 Upon Commodore John Barry.

BARRY or JONES

"Father of the United States Navy"
Historical Reconnaissance

By

LEO GREGORY FINK

Philadelphia

JEFFERIES & MANZ, INC.

2415 East York Street

1962

NIHIL OBSTAT: Joseph P. McClain, C.M.
                           Censor Librorum

IMPRIMATUR: †Joseph McShea, D.D.
                           Bishop of Allentown

Allentown, Penna.
September 13th 1962

The Nihil Obstat and Imprimatur are a declaration that
a book or pamphlet is considered to be free from doctrinal
or moral error. It is not implied that those who have
granted the Nihil Obstat and Imprimature agree with
the contents, opinions or statements expressed.

Contents

(9)

ILLUSTRATIONS

The Honorable CLARE GERALD FENERTY
Pennsylvania Judge, Naval Officer and Barry Orator, 1896–1952

Dedication

to

The Honorable

CLARE GERALD FENERTY

American Catholic Orator

The purpose of this Dedication is obvious. The author of this monograph entitled "BARRY or JONES— Father of the American Navy" has urged me to dedicate his historical work to our mutual friend CLARE GERALD FENERTY as the eloquent "Defender of Catholicism" and America's distinctive orator on the subject of "BARRY—Father of the American Navy."

The Honorable Clare Gerald Fenerty, Judge of the Court of Common Pleas in Philadelphia, was one of the best known Catholic laymen in the United States. He was born in 1896 in Philadelphia and St. Joseph's High School and College laid well the foundations for his professional career. His sudden death as a result of a coronary occlusion occurred in July 1952. The impact of his life upon us has been that of one of the world's golden-tongued orators who renewed the face of the earth with Pentecostal fire and Chrysostomian eloquence.

When Judge Fenerty received in 1952 the "Man of the Year Award," the notable assembly of prominent persons included the Judges of the Supreme Court, Common Pleas Court, Municipal Court, representatives of the Mayor, the District Attorney's Office, City Officials, officials of banks, labor, education, business and representatives of the Federal Government as well as the clergy of all denominations. Philadelphia truly honored her illustrious son! His life was proven as one of service—

whether at sea with the United States Navy in two world wars or in serving of his fellow Americans as teacher, writer in prose and poetry, orator, lawyer, District Attorney, Member of Congress and Judge.

More than fifty years ago, we met Clare Gerald Fenerty for the first time. We were with him in high school and college and ever since maintained a friendship which has been enriched through the years by supporting the same causes.

At both high school and college young Fenerty was a source of amazement to his classmates and of admiration to his professors. He seldom, if ever, got below a 95 percentage in any subject, and his ability to read, translate and speak Latin, Greek and French was extraordinary. He could take any subject and on it acquit himself very well. His poetry—even in the French language—was exceeded only by the beauty of his prose, and his histrionic ability was always recognized by his being chosen for leading roles in such plays as "Oedipus Rex" and others of the ancient classics. Then as a debater and orator he won award after award in class, college, city and state competition—for his great ability. All in all, he had an exceptionally brilliant mind, a capacity for grasping fundamentals readily and a personality that, aside from his intellectuality, won him friends. It is unnecessary to state that from early youth his knowledge of, adherence to and inculcation of Catholicity was consistent, enthusiastic and exemplary.

His two years in the House of Representatives were outstanding. His addresses in Congress in defense of the persecuted Church in Mexico—particularly his criticism of Calles—reached an all-time high in legislative circles and attracted widespread attention. His address in Congress, in 1935, demanding, in a resolution, that the then President Roosevelt break relations with Soviet Russia "because that nation has violated every pledge made in the pact of 1933, is a foe of human freedom and a threat to our nation's future," was indeed prophetic. His militant and successful demand for the re-opening of the Cramps shipyards in Philadelphia restored jobs to thousands of workers. In the same year he introduced bills to prevent the United States from having reciprocal trade agreements with any nation indulging in racial or religious persecution; to make Barry Day and Pulaski Day national holidays; to have foreign nations pay World War debts by the cession of their possessions in the Western Hemisphere to the United States and other measures which, if adopted, would have helped to prevent World War II.

Although possessing a fine record of public service at Washington, Judge Fenerty was defeated for re-election by a few hundred votes. A year later we, with a group of other friends, were pleased to recommend to the then Governor Arthur G. James of Pennsylvania that he appoint Judge Fenerty to a vacancy in the Court of Common Pleas, which is next in standing to the Supreme Court in that State. Governor James did so. The Judge was re-elected for ten years in 1941 and in 1951 was again re-elected, this time unanimously, for he was indorsed by all parties—the only one of 300 candidates, including 15 judges, to win a bi-partisan nomination in the State. His knowledge of the law made him not only a competent judge but won the admiration of the Bar all over the State. His studious habits, his religious outlook helped make his record eminent, but his judicial career was also characterized by hard work. One day, with the temperature in the court at 96, he settled the forty cases on his docket and then dictated letters for several hours to his secretary, Miss Margaret McAteer, suggesting that she leave and transcribe them the next day. Such was his integrity, ability, personality and diligence, that his fellow judges, as one, were visibly moved by his passing.

Messages of sympathy to the family poured in from all parts of the world, including a cable of condolence from Prime Minister Eamon de Valera of Ireland.

The Judge was given many talents, but it can be said he returned them to his Maker. He was staunchly Catholic, was militant in his loyalty to the Church and could always be found adhering to Catholic policy and practice. American to the core, he continually demonstrated that the enemies of religion were the enemies of our nation.

Readers of THE TABLET will recall some of his magnificent addresses. His ringing speech at the Frank Fay rally in Madison Square Garden, January 4, 1946, was oratory at its finest. THE TABLET carried the text of the address, entitled "The Red War on Religion," and then, in order to satisfy the demand, printed 10,000 copies of it in pamphlet form. The requests continued for months and in the end over 100,000 copies of the speech had been circulated. His addresses at the Knights of Columbus Independence Day rally here in 1932, at the anti-Communist rally in the Brooklyn Academy of Music in 1936, at the rally in Elmhurst in defense of Archbishop Stepinac in 1947 and at numerous Communion-Breakfasts and other events will be recalled by many.

We particularly remember two others of his speeches. One given about 22 years ago at the Bishop Molloy Retreat League dinner, when Msgr. Sheen was the other speaker, was a particularly scintillating performance. His thoughts poured out as the mountain stream, leaping and breaking bounds, carrying all before them in his torrential eloquence. Then in his peroration he recited the names of every city from San Antonio to St. Louis to San Francisco, from St. Joseph to St. John, carrying a Saint's name; then he did the same with the rivers and in picturesque language asked how any person could say our forefathers, our nation's pioneers and pathfinders were secularists or un-Christian.

Another speech we vividly recall was given at the Convention Hall in Philadelphia in behalf of Archbishop Stepinac. The late Cardinal Dougherty presided, over 20,000 filled the hall and from 30,000 to 40,000 stood in the streets. The indictment of Tito was masterly, as well as factual, and the moving eloquence utilized in describing the jailed Archbishop left an indelible impress on everyone present. Later Cardinal Dougherty, in telling us of some of the most impressive things in his life, cited this address as an outstanding event and he described it as "oratory at its finest, eloquence greater than any I have heard in my lifetime."

We have heard many orators from the time of William Jennings Bryan and Bourke Cockran to the present, but we believe Judge Fenerty equaled any, for with his magnificent diction, his beautiful word pictures, his humor and irony, his easy flowing prose and magnetic delivery, he had the ring of sincerity which doubly emphasized the truths he was propounding and the earnestness which showed he believed everything he uttered. It is no wonder he was invited to speak in practically every State in the Union.

The deceased layman was an ardent reader of THE TABLET and thought as we did on nearly all current problems. He quoted from these columns regularly and secured for THE TABLET many readers. We shall always hold him, his work, his character and friendship deep in our heart. That such a man should be taken in these difficult days is a tragedy. His loss was widely felt, particularly by his dear ones, the members of his own family, yet throughout the nation the thousands he instructed, inspired, interested and aroused were shocked by his death. The one compensation we have is that in his all too brief life he did incalculable good which will live long after him. With his passing we recalled the words of St. Paul to Timothy: "I have fought the good fight, I have finished the course, I have kept the faith." May Clare Gerald Fenerty, who manifested true greatness, rest in peace eternal!

The dedication of this book to Clare Gerald Fenerty coincidently marks the Tenth Anniversary of his death. Amongst the many facets of his life we find him to be an ardent champion of historical truth and especially in his studies, research and eloquent defense of John Barry as the true and historical "Father of the American Navy." Hundreds of thousands of Catholics and non-Catholics heard him speak on the subject of Barry and to him the author of this book gives much credit for inspiration in writing this historical memorial to perpetuate the truth concerning Barry. We know that the oratorical battles fought by Judge Fenerty in the defense of Barry have motivated the presentation of this new book.

May this dedication of Monsignor Fink's book to our mutual friend in life and death be provocative of the reader's greater interest in the pursuit of historical truth.

PATRICK F. SCANLAN, K.G.S.
Managing Editor

The Brooklyn Tablet
July 4th, 1962
Brooklyn, N. Y.

Prologue

It was at the grave of my grandfather that I knelt before the Cross and the American Flag and there it was that I asked God, the triumphant Leader of the Church Militant, that I might some day serve in the fighting forces of America. My petition was granted in World War I and thus in our patriotic home the Civil War and World War I were forever united. The opportunities of an army chaplain were many and in addition to my spiritual and educational work, I found ample time to delve into the depths of American history which in turn I injected in all my addresses and instructions to the men committed to my care. My grandfather had been wounded in the Battle of Antietam and lost the sight of one eye. The darkness which he suffered gave me vision to see the light of historical truth and my life was dedicated to God and America. This monograph is only one of many personal historical projects which the author found useful in promoting genuine American citizenship amongst those with whom he came in contact in time of war and peace.

Many books have been written on the subject of Barry and Jones. They are not always controversial. In some instances they are partisan and partial to one but forgetful of the other. In other books, the authors are given to fantasy and their imaginations run forth into extavagances which render their writing untruthful. In some public addresses emphasis has been placed upon minor events and attempts have been made to glorify the defects of morality and prescind from the justificaton of an ethical life. Where crass ignorance or bigotry enters into the mind of a speaker or writer, we can expect "a conspiracy of silence" concerning historical truth. As an example of the purposeful suppression of historical truth, we can refer the reader to an address delivered by Captain Richmond Pearson Hobson, U.S.N., on Flag Day, 1901, at the Buffalo Pan-American Exposition, when he said "we captured from the British over 800 vessels and more than 1200 seamen, and of these more than 100 were war vessels of the Royal Navy carrying more than 2,500 guns, while the American losses were scarcely more than one-sixth those of the British." Nevertheless, when he looked "over the range of our Naval history, saw a long line of majestic figures whose very names are an inspiration," he did not, in giving the names of 21 of these majestic figures, include Captain John Barry—the very Father of the American Navy. He was not mentioned amongst those whom "History with her bright and luminous pencil inscribed upon the glorious scroll." Later on this man who purposely omitted the name of Barry became a member of Congress from Alabama.

The legendary life of Jones as portrayed by Augustus C. Buell's "JONES—Father of American Navy" deserved the castigations by Mrs. Reginal deKoven in her "Life and Times of John Paul Jones." Rear Admiral Samuel F. Morison, U.S.N. in his documented and masterful book "JOHN PAUL JONES—A Sailor's Biography" says that Buell is not "the father of lies," but that "his-two-volume biography, which first appeared in 1900, tells more of them than all other writers put together." Since Buell's work has mislead so many educators, authors, orators on patriotic occasions and the producers of modern moving pictures, the erudite and critical Admiral Morrison suggests that librarians should reclassify Buell's books as fiction and not history. Thus either by the suppression of truth or the fabrication of heroic acts, Jones has been glorified and Barry has been neglected and his pre-eminence unjustifiably suppressed. The histories used in many schools are a veritable testimony of this statement. Confusion, therefore, is the legacy which Buell and others have left to a future generation of Americans who wish to know the truth.

The official entombment of John Paul Jones beneath the Chapel of the Naval Academy at Annapolis does not make him the only naval hero of the War for American Independence nor does it proclaim him "Father of the American Navy!" We could easily dismiss the literary and symbolical paternity of the American Navy by assigning, as some writers have proposed, the title of "Father of the American Navy" to General George Washington. However that would not end the discussion which the enemies of Barry started.

We shall *psychoanalyze* the personalities of Jones and Barry and form our conclusions with "malice towards none and justice for all." We shall study their achievements through the *bifocals* of comparative American History; we shall justly understand the differentials of their personalities and see why the non-Catholic Rear Admiral Morison, U.S.N., called Barry "the most popular captain in the Navy," why the staunch non-Catholic physician and author, Dr. Benjamin Rush, M.D., wrote Barry's eulogy and epitaph which contain these words "he bore an early and active part as a Captain in the Navy and afterwards became its Commander-in-Chief," and why the cultured historian and television cicerone, Mrs. Jacqueline Kennedy, in leading millions of people through the White House at Washington eloquently described one of the historical paintings as that of Commodore John Barry "Father of the American Navy."

We hope that this book dedicated to the Honorable Clare Gerald Fenerty—eloquent Philadelphia Judge and Champion of Commodore Barry, by the prolific writer and editor of the Brooklyn Tablet—Patrick F. Scanlan, K.S.G.—will unite more historians in the common objective of rendering historical justice to Commodore Barry.

BARRY or JONES—who was Father of the American Navy? You, dear reader and philosopher should know the truth! You must judge this matter for yourself! Let the differentials of American History reveal in the mirror of justice the truth and nothing but the truth!

Yours for God and America,

Right Reverend Monsignor

LEO GREGORY FINK
P.A., V.G., LL.D., Litt.D.
Chaplain, 212 Eng., 12th Div., U.S.A.

BARRY DAY
September 13th 1962
Sacred Heart Church
Allentown, Pa.

CHAPTER I

Genesis of the Two American Seamen

The comparative genesis of John Barry and John Paul Jones is interesting for Americans who are intrigued by the truths contained in the Colonial history of the United States of America. The citizen who has proven his love for God and America by actual service in the armed forces, knows full well the inspiration which he obtains from the factual records and achievements of our national heroes. The apochryphal interpollations of some unscrupulous writers or the conspiracy of silence manifested in some history is to be expected. Writers who either innocently or intentionally transmit to posterity "half-truths," do so under the influence or pressures which are political or religious. Truth may be proclaimed after a process of time and impartial inquiry, but the whole truth is tardily accepted by a new generation which had been virtually steeped in sedation, prejudice and ignorance. The canards of the past linger on and are ofttimes impregnated into the minds of generations yet unborn.

The author has no intention of recording anything else but historical truth, and in so doing, he hopes to entertain the reader of this monograph as well as satisfy the philosopher—the lover of wisdom—who will only be satisfied with the unvarnished and unadulterated facts concerning John Barry and John Paul Jones. Our words concerning the birth and adolescent days of these two American seamen shall be brief, so that we can dwell with particular emphasis upon the real achievements which made them famous, and the historical differentials which claimed for both of them the encomium of "Father of the American Navy."

1745

John Barry was born in Ireland in the year 1745. The place of his birth was Tachumshain, County Wexford, Barony of Forth, and the place of his baptism was Lady Island Church where Reverend Father James French performed the ceremony. The Parish Church Register gives the names of James and Ellen Barry as his parents. The boyhood of Barry was spent at Rostoonstown, where he enjoyed the pleasures and endured the hardships of the fishermen. Upon the "Lochs" or lakes, he received his first experiences in navigation and the language of his primary education was "neither good English nor good Irish"—the dialect of Forth. He arrived in Philadelphia in the year 1760 with the intention of a permanent residence in America.

1747

John Paul (to whom the name Jones was later added) was born in Scotland in the year 1747. The place of his birth was Arbigland, in the Parish of Kirkbean and the Stewartry of Kirkoudbright. His parents were John Paul and Jean Macduff Paul, who were Presbyterians. As a boy, John Paul launched his "fairy frigate" on the shores of Solway; his education he received in the Parish school of Kirkbean; and through his occasional visits to Whitehaven, he received a strong relish for the sea which led him later to accept an apprenticeship at Whitehaven where he applied himself to the theory of navigation and certain forms of a liberal education. His first voyage to the open seas he made before he was thirteen years of age, in the ship "Friendship" of Whitehaven with Captain Benson. The ship was bound for the Rappahannock in America and it gave John Paul an opportunity of visiting his brother who had previously settled in Virginia.

In 1766 he saw service on the ship "Two Friends" enroute to Jamaica, and also served on the frigates "John" and the "Betsy" of London enroute to the West Indies. In the year 1771, Jones left Scotland and arrived in America in the year 1773. He temporarily settled in Virginia with the intention of administering his brother's estate and pursuing the rural life in America. His plans failed and when Congress at the conclusion of the year 1775 attempted to form the first "naval force" or Navy, John Paul espoused the cause of the colonists in their battle for independence from British rule.

Both Barry and Jones faced three splendid opportunities, namely,

1st: Service in the American Merchant Marine

2nd: Service in founding the American or United States Navy.

3rd: Naval Service against Britain for American Independence.

CHAPTER II

Captain Barry and Lieutenant Jones
December 7th 1775

It was rumored in Colonial Days that John Barry left Ireland without informing his friends and sailed to the Island of Jamaica from which he came directly to Philadelphia in the year 1760. His friends knew of his early enthusiasm and love for America. He found employment with Mr. Willing of the shipping firm of Willing, Meredith and Cadwallader, and lived with the family of General Cadwallader. This close association with prominent business men of Philadelphia gave him the needed prestige of an enterprising and ambitious seaman. The busy street upon which the shipping firm converged was the present Willing's Alley between Third and Fourth Street south of Walnut Street and stood at the head of the well known landmark Dock Creek which emptied into the Delaware River. The famous and historical church of "Old Saint Joseph's" was built on Willing's Alley in the year 1732 by the Jesuit Missionaries.

Barry's first important position was that of Captain of the "Barbadoes," a schooner of 62 tons which sailed from Philadelphia on October 2nd 1766; on May 30th 1771, he took over the "Patty and Polly;" on September 2nd 1771, he commanded the "Frugality;" on October 24th 1771, he was Captain of the "Industry" rated at 45 tons; the "Peggy" of 25 tons he also commanded on October 14th 1771, and finally he witnessed his old ship "The Black Prince" being sold by its owners to the Continental Congress. This same ship was renamed the "Alfred" after King Alfred the Great, who was reputed to be the

Ship Building on the Delaware

founder of the British Navy. It was taken over by Captain Salstonstall and became the flagship of Captain Esek Hopkins—the first Commodore or Admiral of the First Fleet sailing under Continental authority.

Barry was assigned as Captain of the "Lexington" directly under the authority of Continental Congress on December 7th 1775, while on the same day, Jones was commissioned as First Lieutenant on the "Alfred" under Captain Salonstall.

The merchant marine service of America was quite active from 1760 to 1775 and Barry was steadily engaged. Jones did not settle permanently in America until 1773 when he began his work from the port of Philadelphia. The need of an American Navy was imperative and both Barry and Jones favored the same as a permanent institution for the welfare and progress of the embryonic nation. When Boston was in the hands of the British in 1775, the colonists naturally desired to cut off all supplies which were being sent in store-ships and also of confiscating powder and munitions of war which were obtainable in the colonies. Hence, "Letters of Marque and Reprisal" were authorized by the General Court of Massachusetts on November 13th 1775 and courts were elected to try and condemn British ships which might be captured. General Washington, as Commander-in-Chief, gave commissions to a number of vessels to intercept British vessels bearing supplies for Boston and on December 13th 1775, Continental Congress approved a report of a committee appointed to plan for the Naval Armament of the Colonies to cruise both the Atlantic Ocean and in the Delaware Bay and River for the purpose of cutting off supplies to Philadelphia where the British were also entrenched. The American Navy was thus of necessity forced into existence and its evolution from private-ships to an organized fleet gave courage to Washington and his struggling military forces.

BARRY	JONES

BARRY

1745–John Barry was born in the town of Tachumshain, County Wexford, Barony of Forth, Ireland. He was baptized in Lady Island Church by Rev. Father James French. His parents were James and Ellen Barry and he spent his boyhood on the lakes at Rostoonstown where many people made their living by fishing.

1760–Barry came to Philadelphia and was employed with shipping firm of Willing, Meredith & Cadwallader.

1766–Served on "Barbadoes."

1770–Served "Industry."
1771–Served "Patty & Polly" and "Frugality."
1774–Served "Peggy"–200 tons.
1775–Served "Black Prince" which was later changed to "Alfred."

1775–Served on "Lexington."
On December 7th, Barry was made officially "Captain" on the "Lexington"—a 14 four pounder vessel purchased by the Marine Committee of Congress and directly under the authority of Continental Congress.
Barry completes 15 years in America.

JONES

1747–John Paul was born at Arbigland, Parish of Kirkbean, Stewartry of Kirkoudbright, Scotland. His parents were John Paul and Jean Macduff Paul. He apprenticed as Seaman in Whitehaven and at 13 visited America aboard the ship "Friendship" to visit his brother in Virginia.

1766–Jones shipped as 3rd Mate on "Two Friends" of Kingston, Jamaica. Engaged in slave traffic. Left boat in West Indies because he was opposed to slave traffic. Returned on Brigantine "John" to Scotland. The Captain and Mate of "John" died of fever but Jones brought the boat safely to Scotland and was made Master by the owners as reward for his excellent seamanship.

1773–Jones arrived in Virginia with intentions to pursue farm life and remain in America. Changed his name from John Paul to John Paul Jones.

1775–Jones hoisted the "Rattlesnake Flag" aboard the "Alfred" off the Walnut Street Wharf, Philadelphia, on Dec. 3rd.
Jones was officially named 1st Lieutenant of the "Alfred" on December 7th. This vessel was formerly the "Black Prince" which Continental Congress purchased. Captain Salonstall commanded the ship under Admiral Ezek Hopkins who made it the flagship of his fleet.
Jones completes 2 years in America.

CHAPTER III

Barry Captures First British Vessel
April 7th 1776

In our endeavor to keep in juxta-position the contemporary activities of Barry and Jones, we find the year 1776 one of intense interest. It was a year in which Barry found favor because of his capture of the British Sloop "Edward" as the first American War Prize on April 7th 1776. It was also the year in which Jones was falsely accused of not doing his duty in the affair of the escape of the British ship "Glasgow" on April 9th 1776. The psychological impact upon the world was great. The first war prize of Barry exhilarated the patriots and the loss or escape of the other ship gave comfort to the enemy. However, in justice to Jones, we shall not condemn him for the escape of the "Glasgow."

In the order of time, beginning with January 1776, we find both Barry and Jones in the Port of Philadelphia. The work of the embryo navy was to be the harassment of all British shipping. Jones was to cover the Atlantic Ocean from Massachusetts to Virginia to intercept British supplies for Boston, while Barry was to patrol the Delaware River against the bringing of military forces and supplies to Philadelphia. On February 17th 1776, Jones sailed out of the Delaware Bay for the Bahamas as his first objective. He was 1st Lieutenant on the "Alfred" under Captain Salonstall with Commander Ezek Hopkins in charge of the fleet. Before sailing out of the Delaware, on December 3rd 1775, Lieutenant Jones unfurled the so-called "rattlesnake Flag" which some writers claim was the Continental "Striped Flag." Later, on January 1st 1776, General Washington at Cambridge unfurled for the first time what was called the "Grand Union Flag" to which the British sloop "Edward" surrendered on April 7th 1776.

In order to clear up some of the meanings of the Continental "Striped Flag," we must remember that officially there was no American Flag until June 14th 1777. The flags which were used in 1775 were many. Every colony had its own flag, captains of armed vessels indulged their fancies and displayed flags with many designs. Therefore, in few words, using the best judgment in the matter of this dispute as to whether Barry or Jones unfurled the first American Flag, let us re-state these claims of priority:

December 3rd 1775:   1st Lieutenant Jones unfurled the "Grand Union Flag" or what was known as the "Rattlesnake Flag" on the flagship "Alfred" off the Walnut Street wharf of Philadelphia. This flag was made of red and white stripes with the symbol of a rattlesnake in the attitude of going to strike, which was in the middle of the flag beneath which were the words "Don't tread on me."

January 1st 1776:   General Washington unfurled for the first time the "Grand Union" or "Continental Flag" which contained red and white stripes and a blue field with a Red Cross placed over St. Andrew's White Cross.

April 7th 1776:   Captain Barry unfurled on his "Lexington" the same flag which Washington used and with this "Union Flag" captured the first British war prize of the Revolution, namely the "Edward." In Probers "History of the American Flag," he says that Barry's "Lexington" was the first vessel that bore the "Continental Flag" to victory on the ocean."

June 14th 1777:   First National Flag designed by Wash-
                    ington and adopted by Continental
                    Congress which contained red and
                    white stripes and a blue field with a
                    circle of 13 stars.

The outstanding capture by Barry of the British sloop
"Edward" was made off the Capes of Virginia where the
"Edward" acted as a tender to the man of war the "Liver-
pool." The ship was brought to Philadelphia with Captain
Bolger and the prisoners taken aboard were detained in a jail
at 6th & Walnut Streets in Philadelphia. The "Edward" was
the first British armed cruiser with 6 guns and a number of
swivels captured under the authority of the Continental Marine
Committee. The date of this important sea victory for the
Colonists was April 7th 1776.

Just two days later, April 9th 1776, the unfortunate escape
of the Glasgow occurred. What are the details in brief?

The squadron under Ezek Hopkins in which Jones was
1st Lieutenant of the "Alfred" was ordered to act against Lord
Dunmore who was ravaging the Atlantic Coast around Virginia. Owing to the ice blockades, the fleet did not leave Cape
Henlopen until February 17th 1776. It first reached Abaco in
the Bahamas and then entered the Port of New Providence and
on March 7th removed all the cannon found in the fort. On
April 9th 1776 the escape of the British ship "Glasgow" occurred which brought Jones into the limelight of the year. We
believe that he was wrongly accused. Here are his own words
in explanation which clear him of personal guilt.

"In the night of April 9th 1776, on the return of the squadron from the Providence expedition, the American arms by sea
were first tried in an action with the "Glasgow," a British
frigate of 24 guns off Block Island. Both the "Alfred" and the
"Columbus" mounted two batteries. The "Alfred" mounted
30, the "Columbus" 28 guns. The first battery was so near the
water as to be fit for nothing, except in a harbor or very smooth
sea. The sea was at times perfectly smooth.

"Mr. Jones was stationed between decks to command the
"Alfred's" first battery, which was well served whenever the
guns should be brought to bear on the enemy, as appears by
the official letter of the commander in chief giving an account
of that action. Mr. Jones therefore did his duty; and as he had
no direction whatever, either of the general disposition of the

squadron, or the sails and helm of the "Alfred," he can stand charged with no part of the disgrace of that night."

The "Glasgow" escaped—that is the truth. The one shot which carried away the steering gear of the "Alfred" was the cause of the trouble. That shot could not have been repeated in a hundred trials, yet the fact remained that the British Frigate of 20 guns had run into the gamut of the American Squadron of 90 guns and had cleverly escaped. The "Glasgow" executed the trick alone, but the British never repeated the trick again by trying to take on 5 vessels. Commander Ezek Hopkins tried to explain the matter and clear Jones of responsibility of the loss, however since Hopkins was old and held in ill repute, the public continued to blame Jones for the escape of the "Glasgow." The argument never ended but if we read the statement of Jones of incidents which occurred immediately after the escape, we can form our own judgement in the matter. Here are the words of Jones: "The squadron steered directly for New London and entered that port two days after the action. Here George Washington lent the squadron 200 men, as was thought, for some enterprize. The squadron, however, stole around to Rhode Island, and up the River to Providence. Here a court-martial was held for the trial of Captain Whipple, for not assisting in the action with the "Glasgow."

"Another court-martial was held for the trial of Captain Hazard, who has been appointed captain of the sloop "Providence" at Philadelphia. Some time after Mr. Jones had refused that command. Captain Hazard was broken and rendered incapable of serving in the navy.

"The next day, the 10th of May 1776, Mr. Jones was ordered by the commander in chief to take command of the "Providence." This proves that Mr. Jones did his duty on the "Providence" expedition. As the commander in chief had in his hands no blank commission, this appointment was written and signed on the back of the commission that Mr. Jones had re-

ceived at Philadelphia, the 7th of December 1775. Captain
Jones had orders to receive on board the "Providence" the
soldiers that had been borrowed from General Washington and
to carry them to New York."

These words convincely show, from Jones own words,
that he was not to be blamed for the escape of the Glasgow and
that he fulfilled his own duties faithfully on that fateful event
of April 9th 1776. Some of his subsequent activities were as
follows: On June 10th 1776, he entered Newport, Rhode
Island, to take a British sloop armed for war, but unfortunately the sloop escaped before Jones arrived. With orders from
the Commander in Chief, Jones went next to Newburyport to
convoy some vessels to Philadelphia; he also convoyed Lieutenant Hackett in the "Fly" with a cargo of cannon into the
sound of New York, and after many hazards of the sea infested
with frigates under Lord Howe, he finally returned to the
Delaware on August 1st 1776.

Then on August 8th 1776 Jones received from the President of Congress the commission of Captain. He left the Delaware on August 21st and arrived in Rhode Island on October
7th 1776 to conduct a campaign against the coal fleet and the
fisheries. At this time, he changed positions from the "Providence" to the "Alfred" as commander on October 22nd 1776.
The "Providence" and the "Alfred" sailed together northward
towards Boston and enroute captured a British Brig laden with
a rich cargo of dry goods, a scow laden with fish and a large
ship "Mellish" armed for war and laden with soldiers' clothing
bound for Canada. With five prize ships laden with valuable
supplies, Jones was attacked by the British frigate "Milford"
which he cleverly out manouvered and finally arrived safely
through storms and hazards into the harbor of Boston on
December 15th 1776. The good news of the capture of the
cargo of soldiers' clothing reached General Washington before
he crossed the Delaware and took the enemies garrison at
Trenton on Christmas 1776.

After the escape of the "Glasgow" on April 9th 1776,
Jones was employed with the above named operations which
showed him to be in good standing. At the same time Barry
was busily engaged and on June 6th 1776 was assigned to the
armed cruiser "Effingham." He captured the British "Lady
Susan" with six 4-pound guns and 25 prisoners and on Sept.
26th he also captured the British "Betsy" a sloop of 50 tons.

On October 18th, the "Lexington" was assigned to Captain
Henry Johnston while Barry took command of the newly built
"Effingham." Little could be accomplished in the upper
Delaware.

With Philadelphia in the hands of the British, some
American ships assembled to the north of Fort Mifflin under
Barry, with the British Navy bottling the south Delaware and
Jones out on the open seas in a campaign of harassment,
General Washington with General Ewing and Cadawalder
planned the crossing of the Delaware. Barry showed his desire
to assist Washington and whilst he was helpless aboard the
"Effingham," he joined the land forces and assisted in the
crossing of the Delaware for the Battle of Trenton and Prince-
ton. With the Marines under Captain Brown, Captain Barry
became an aide to General Cadwalader and also to General
Washington. The versatility of Barry was a good reason for his
popularity amongst all people engaged in the fight for freedom.
Both seaman and soldier, Barry risked his life for the cause of
American Liberty!

CHAPTER IV

Barry Crosses Delaware With Washington
December 25th 1776

It was General Cornwallis, the defeated British Commander, who once said that General Washington's brightest laurels in history would not be found along the shores of the Chesapeake Bay but near to the humble crossing of a Delaware River Ferry which Washington used to obtain his victory at Trenton and gloriously turn the tide of the American Revolution. The words of Thomas Paine, Colonial patriot, soldier and writer, have often been applied to the dark December of 1776 when Washington and his ill-clad and starving soldiers camped along the western shores of the Delaware near McKonkey's Ferry: "These are the times that try men's souls. The summer soldiers and sunshine patriots will, in this crisis, shrink from the service of his country, but he that stands it now deserves the love and thanks of man and woman."

In the darkness of Christmas, 1776, orders from General Washington set the American Army into action. This is well described by one of the officers:

> Six P.M. The regiments have had their evening parade, but instead of returning to their quarters are marching toward the Ferry. It is fearfully cold and raw and a snowstorm is setting in. The wind is northeast and beats in the faces of the men. It will be a terrible night for the men who have no shoes. Some of them have tied old rags around their feet, others are barefoot, but I have never heard a man complain. They are ready to suffer any hardship and die rather than give up their liberty.

During the storm of sleet and snow and darkness, Washington directed the preparatory work for crossing the ice-bound Delaware. Colonel Knox commanded the boatmen, while Captain Blunt timed the crossing of each and every boatload of soldiers. Colonel Glover's regiment of former fishermen and sailors from Marblehead, Mass., rowed the boats through the icejammed river to the Jersey shores. Washington was also supposed to have been assisted by other Generals who would unite in the attack upon Trenton, but General Cadwalader and General Ewing found it impossible to cross the stream at Bristol and Trenton, while Washington actually crossed the river at McKonkey's Ferry.

There was only one "Kindly Light" which shone in the midst of the encircling gloom. There was only one objective—Liberty or Death! The War of Independence was a struggle for both the soldier and the civilian. Doubt, indecision and betrayal oft times threatened the ideals of American Freedom. The following extract vividly portray the actual ordeal of the Colonists who believed in Washington's ideal of Liberty or Death!

"The timid, the faint-hearted, the treacherous were fast accepting British allegiance. Even heretofore stalwart hearts wavered in the cause of liberty. The newly proclaimed Independence of hot July, 1776, the threat of defiance to England's tyranny, was now in the chill December of 1776, like the earth about to be sheathed in the coldness of death. The alarm came to Philadelphia. Shops were shut, schools closed and the inhabitants engaged solely in providing for the defense of the city, now the aim of the enemy. But out of this gloom and alarm came the "Crossing of the Delaware" and the "Victory of Trenton!"

We well understand why Bucks County is proud of its historical heritage! As Tertullian, the historian, once said of primitive Christianity—"in the blood of martyrs the seed of Christianity was sown"—so also could it be said that in the blood of Washington soldiers, the seed of American patriotism was sown in Bucks County of Pennsylvania!

As Catholics, we are naturally interested in the part played by Catholic patriots in Washington's crossing of the Delaware. It has often been emphasized that Colonel Glover's regiment of sea-faring sailors and fishermen of Marblehead, Massachusetts, manned the boats across the ice-jammed Delaware River, but often little is said about the procurement of the boats from Patrick Colvin, the only Catholic resident in Trenton who was interested in the Cause of the Patriots and helped to furnish boats for Washington on December 25, 1776, in order to cross the river at no other point than McKonkey's Ferry. The words of Washington assure us of his personal recognition of the part played by Catholics in the American Revolution and his full appreciation of Catholic loyalty can be found in his memorable words, "your fellow citizens will not forget the patriotic part which you took in the accomplishment of their Revolution and the Establishment of their Government, or the important assistance which they received from a nation (France) in which the Roman Catholic Religion is professed. May the members of your Society in America, animated alone by the pure spirit of Christianity and still conducting themselves as the faithful subjects of our free Government, enjoy every temporal and spiritual felicity."

One of the outstanding patriots and "fighting Catholics" who was near to the heart of Washington at the time of the Crossing of the Delaware, was Captain Barry, the Father of the American Navy, who organized a Company of Volunteers and went to Washington's assistance on the shores of the Delaware. In co-operation with Captain William Brown he lent efficient service in transporting the army for the Battle of Trenton. Captain

Barry also rated as an aide to General Cadwalader and also
brought the baggage of the captured Hessians, as well as
that of the surgeons and physicians, to Princeton. What
an admirable service was rendered by Barry the Catholic,
who when he had no ship to fight upon, he marched with
the militia through Bucks County en route to the Battle of
Trenton! When Philadelphia was taken over by the
British and American hopes were at their lowest ebb, the
British General Lord Howe made a flattering offer to
Barry to desert Washington but Barry's reply will ever
remain in these memorable words: "Not the value and
command of the whole British Fleet can lure me from the
cause of my country."

Since we have accentuated the part played by Commodore Barry on the high seas and upon the consecrated
shores of the Delaware River, it will not be amiss to inter-
polate an abstract from the Historian Martin I. J.
Griffin's writings concerning the Father of the American
Navy and his presence with General Washington along
the Delaware River.

"The upper Delaware was now the center of action and
the place where God's providence would be so strikingly
manifested on that cold Christmas night of 1776.

"Captain Barry at once recruited a company of
volunteers for service on land. Doubtless many of his crew
stood by him in this new line of endeavor for freedom.
Those were indeed perilous times, 'the times that tried
men's souls.' Barry was equal to the emergency when
Washington was forced to exclaim in that despairing wail:
'In ten days this army will have ceased to exist. . . . We
are at the end of our tether!' All seemed lost. The hour of
defeat, dismay and destruction was about to strike. The
timid, the faint-hearted, the treacherous were fast going
over to British allegiance. 'At last the old fox (Washing-
on) is in a trap,' said Cornwallis. A day's freezing of the
waters of the Delaware would bring the complete destruc-

tion of the 'rebel army.' Why not sit down and, amid Christmas festivity, wait nature's alliance in the waters? Why harass Hessians by building boats and rafts to cross to the other side? There need be no concern nor haste— 'the fox is in the trap.' That Declaration of Independence proclaimed in hot July as a concentrated threat and defiance to tyranny, as well as earth's noblest resolve for freedom, would in a brief six months be like Nature's garb this chill December—cold as in death.

"Philadelphia was in alarm for its safety. The Pennsylvania Council of Safety on December 2nd, ordered to be distributed this broadside:

RESOLVED, THAT IT IS THE OPINION OF THIS BOARD, THAT ALL THE SHOPS IN THIS CITY BE SHUT UP, THAT THE SCHOOLS BE BROKE UP, AND THE INHABITANTS ENGAGE SOLELY IN PROVIDING FOR THE DEFENCE OF THE CITY, AT THIS TIME OF EXTREME DANGER. BY ORDER OF COUNCIL, DAVID RITTENHOUSE, VICE-PRESIDENT.

"Out of the gloom came the Victory at Trenton.

"To the Colonial cause had been given the man who was to lead the people out of bondage and through the desert to security and peace to the land of freedom. Look through all the writings of Washington in all the days of the mighty struggle, and see how firm and strong was his faith in the justice of the cause and his reliance on Divine Providence in 'the times that tried men's souls' as the crisis of December '76 was described by a man of little faith, the pamphleteer of the Revolution, Thomas Paine. Brave men who stood by Washington amid the disasters in the Jerseys were tried; and no less so were the noble-hearted ones beyond the lines. But in that dark hour, when all seemed lost, Thomas FitzSimons, a merchant, and Captain Barry, a seaman, one in faith as they were one in country of nativity, were now one in endeavor for their adopted land. They hastened to the aid of Washington on the banks of the Delaware above Trenton. And when Washington crossed the ice-blocked river these two Philadelphia Catholics did the duty of patriots and heroes in the strife that won the victories at Trenton and Princeton. They went to the front, each with a company, to uphold the Declaration of Independence, when all who had pledged 'their lives, their fortunes and sacred honor,' excepting the lone Quaker John Dickinson, had fled beyond the immediate reach of British power; and, but for the Militia of Pennsylvania, might in the general wreck and carnage made by that power have left the full force of its vindictiveness.'

"Though the month began in gloom, if not terror, the year 1776, closed with victory animating all Patriots. The Navy had 342 British vessels captured to its credit for the year. Not among the laggards or inefficient had been Captain John Barry. A million sterling in goods had been taken from the enemy by the American cruisers according to the estimate of Benjamin Franklin, in October, when he wrote: 'Nothing will give us greater weight and importance in the eyes of the commercial States than a conviction that we can annoy, on occasion, their trade and carry our prizes into safe harbors' (Am. Ar. 5-2-1245).

"Who more active during all of 1776, and thus giving 'weight and importance' abroad to the endeavor being made for Freedom, for who so near the rebel capital— Philadelphia, did more to annoy British trade and carry prizes to safe harbors than Captain John Barry.

"Captain John Barry, as we have seen, with a company of volunteers in December 1776, took part in the Trenton Campaign. In co-operstion with the marines under Captain William Brown, he lent efficient service in transporting Washington's army across the Delaware, when they took part in the battles of Trenton and Princeton (2d Pa. Ar. 1 p. 20, 234). The marines remained until the 23rd of January.

"On that day Washington wrote from Middlebrook to General Joseph Reed: 'The spirited manner in which the militia of Pennsylvania turned out upon the late maneuvre of the enemy has, in my opinion, given shock to the enemy greater than any event which has happened in the course of this dispute, because it was altogether unexpected and gave the decisive stroke to the enterprise on Philadelphia' (Ford's Writings of Washington, Vol. V p. 196). The minutes of the Pennsylvania Board of War, under date of March 27th, 1777, record: 'Mr. Moses Young was directed to pay Jesse How £6, 19.9 for the use of the volunteers in Captain Barry's Company when going to camp in December last; to be charged to Congress" (Pa. Arch. 2nd series Vol. 1 p. 20).

"Captain Barry, in service in New Jersey, acted as an aide to General Cadwalader, and as such became, on one occasion of which there is record, an aide to Washington on special service, as shown by the American Commander-in-chief's answer to a request made by General Lord Cornwallis.

"Writing from Morristown on January 8, 1777, after giving assurance that relief convoy bringing assistance to the Hessians taken and wounded at Trenton and Princeton would not be molested by his regular soldiers, but that he could not answer for the militia, who were 'exceedingly exasperated at the treatment they have met with from both Hessians and British troops,' Washington said: "I therefore thought it most desirable to direct Captain Barry, the bearer of this, to give a safe conduct to the Hessian baggage as far as Philadelphia and the surgeon and medicines to Princeton' (Spark's Writings of Washington IV p. 268). On Barry's return to Philadelphia after the Trenton Campaign, he engaged in defense Naval preparations for the protection of Philadelphia."

"Commodore John Barry" by Martin I. J. Griffin
Philadelphia 1903, p. 44 to 48

From the words of Dr. Benjamin Rush, non-Catholic and one of the signers of the Declaration of Independence we can understand that Barry was heart and soul American and that when John Paul Jones left America and went to Paris for pleasure and to Russia for service in Queen Catherine's Navy, Captain Barry remained in America in the service of his adopted country until death. The beloved physician of the Revolution, Dr. Benjamin Rush, said of Barry: "America was the object of Barry's Patriotism and the theatre of his usefulness in the Revolutionary War which established the Independence of the United States."

Reconnaissance

BARRY	JONES
1776–Jan. 15th Barry assisted Commodore Hopkins in preparation of voyage to the Bahamas. March 14th–Barry Captain of "Lexington."	1776–Lieutenant Jones remained 6 weeks at Reedy Island frozen by ice to the shore. Prepared to sail against Lord Dunmore in Virginia and later joined by small ships and schooner from Baltimore.
March 17th–Hopkins sailed from New Providence and brought with him the Governor and others as hostages with military stores and ammunition. General Washington on same day entered Boston during the forced evacuation by the British. Barry was active on the	Feb. 17th–Sailed out of Delaware Bay for the Bahamas and anchored at Abaco and later entered the harbor of New Providence. March 7th–Embarked the can-

Reconnaissance

BARRY	JONES
Delaware River promoting Naval Activities conducive to the formation of the American Navy.	non found in Fort at Nassau harbor.

BARRY

Delaware River promoting Naval Activities conducive to the formation of the American Navy.

March 23rd–Congress ordered "Letters of Marque" and authorized public and private cruisers to capture British vessels or to seize or destroy supplies for British Naval Forces.

March 25th–Barry on the "Lexington" anchored off Cape May, N. J.

April 7th–First battle off the Capes of Virginia. Barry captured the British sloop "Edward" and brought it to Philadelphia. This was the first armed cruiser captured under the authority of Continental Marine Committee. Vessel had 6 guns a number of swivels and a crew of 25 prisoners.

May 8th–Barry on the "Hornet" patrolled the Delaware River and supplied men for other ships in the Delaware while the "Lexington" was being repaired. Barry in command of the "Lexington" protects 13 ships being built in Philadelphia.

May 31st–Barry went to sea bearing the Union or Continental Flag which Washington furled at Cambridge on January 1st 1776. The "Roebuck"

JONES

non found in Fort at Nassau harbor.

April 9th–Incident of "Glasgow" and its escape become controversial charge against Jones. The "Alfred" attempted to capture the "Glasgow," fired upon it, encircled it and crippled it, but it escaped. Jones explained his part in the affair, saying that he was not in control or command of the "Alfred" but stationed on the lower gun-deck during the action. The commander thought it imprudent to pursue the "Glasgow" and did not wish to lose the prizes he had taken in battle. He did not wish to be decoyed by the enemy and therefore ceased to pursue the "Glasgow" with the result that it escaped.

Because of the bitter dispute over the escape of the "Glasgow," Lieut. Jones was replaced in command of the "Alfred" by Captain Hinman on January 14th 1777.

Contradictory to this penalty, Jones was made commander of the "Providence," and Jones therefore declared himself innocent but public sentiment was divided.

May 10th–Jones was officially placed in command of the "Providence" as Captain.

Reconnaissance

BARRY

British man of war and her tender "Edward" put out to sea in pursuit of the "Lexington" but Barry was too swift and eluded the enemy.

June 6th–Barry assigned to cruiser "Effingham" which was armoured.

August 2nd–Barry captured "Lady Susan" British vessel armed with 6 four pound carriage guns with 25 prisoners.

Sept. 26th–Barry captured "Betsy" British sloop of 50 tons.

Oct. 18th–"Lexington" given to Captain Henry Johnston while Barry assumed command of newly built "Effingham"

Dec. 24th–Barry organized volunteers to assist Washington in crossing of the Delaware. With the Marines under Captain Brown, Barry became an aide to General Cadawalder and the records show that he was also an aide to General Washington and safely brought the baggage of the captured Hessians as well as all the materials of the surgeons and physicians of Princeton.
General Washington's crossing of the Delaware brought joy and comfort to American colonists. Barry was with Washington in defeat and victory.

JONES

June 10th: In Rhode Island.

June 13th–Convoyed boats with ammunition.

August 1st—Jones in Delaware River.

August 8th–Jones commissioned as Captain of "Providence" with orders to cruise against the enemy.

August 21st–Jones left Delaware River area for open seas.

Oct. 7th–Arrived at Rhode Island. Captured 16 prizes in in 6 weeks and destroyed small vessels and fishery. Expedition against Coal Fleet off Cape Breton followed.

Oct. 22nd–Jones in command of "Alfred."
Nov. 2nd–Jones in command of "Alfred" and the "Providence" passed between the enemies frigates at Block Island and anchored near Nantucket.

Nov. 16th–Jones captured a brig off Louisbourg laden with rich cargo of dry goods, a scow laden with fish and a large ship "Mellish" bound for Canada, armed for war and laden with soldiers' clothing.

Nov. 24th–Jones captured 3 ships of the Coal Fleet con-

Reconnaissance

BARRY	JONES
"The brightest laurels of Washington were gathered from the banks of the Delaware, rather from those of the Chesapeake." In the crises of faith and in the hour of victory, Barry was with General Washington.	voyed by the frigate "Flora" and captured also another ship rich laden from Liverpool. Dec. 7th–Jones fell in with Frigate "Milford" on edge of St. George's bank. Dec. 15th–The "Mellish" arrived safely with the soldiers' clothing at Dartmouth. Jones arrived in Boston. News of the supply of clothing reached General Washington before he crossed the Delaware to Trenton.

CHAPTER V

British Burn 21 Vessels — Washington in
Valley Forge 1777-1778

It was General Washington who emulated David and cried out as he knelt in the snows of Valley Forge "Out of the depths have I cried to Thee, O Lord! Lord! hear my voice!" Washington prayed for victory and independence, but during the years 1777 and 1778 he experienced his greatest sorrow. Surrounded by a few true friends, who believed in Independence from British rule, Washington reviewed the miseries and confused philosophy of his people.

The impact of British naval and military forces was seriously felt in Philadelphia. Barry had been named to defend the port of Philadelphia, for he was the Senior Commander of the Navy in the port of Philadelphia in the month of February 1777. When Washington gave orders for all American vessels to anchor north of Market Street, there were twenty one vessels burned and destroyed in the Delaware by the vindictive British. Amongst these vessels was Barry's "Effingham" which had under Washington's orders been buried in the mud banks of the Delaware but retrieved by the British and burned on May 6th 1778. Fort Mifflin itself was attacked and the construction of new vessels was placed in serious jeopardy.

The greatest humiliation of all was the occupation of Philadelphia by the British which lasted until June 18th 1778. American Independence and its defense were at a low ebb. The Liberty Bell was removed from Philadelphia and secretly hidden within the walls of Zion Evangelical Reformed Church of Allentown, Penna., and safeguarded during the period of Washington's Retreat at Valley Forge of 1777 and 1778. Refugees from Philadelphia, among which was Barry's wife, sought asylum and protection in Reading, Pennsylvania. By some historians the years 1777 and 1778 were thought to be the nadir of the American Revolution.

The valorous attempts of Lafayette, DuPortail, DeKalb, Pulaski, Kosciusko and other military leaders from foreign countries were not as successful as we might surmize, for intrigue and internal dissension combined with the many insolent attempts of the British to bribe these men to desert General Washington. In addition to the serious destruction by fire and sword, there was in reality a "cold war" raging amongst the thirteen original colonies. The differentials between the Americans who wanted "Independence from England" and those who simply desired "Liberty under King George" were confusing as to their philosophy and religion. Confusion reigned supreme and the work of Washington as a peacemaker was an arduous task. To the credit of such men as Charles Carroll of Carrollton, who was the wealthiest man and a Catholic, who openly stated his reasons for signing the Declaration of Independence and taking side with Washington with the prospect of losing his entire fortune and even his life, the motive was not liberty under British rule, but Independence from England.

When the laws of the Province of Maryland were changed by England and religious liberty was opposed, many Catholics sought sanctuary in Pennsylvania. The Catholics who remained in Maryland were naturally opposed to England and hoped to obtain religious liberty through Independence from England. Therefore, they took sides with Washington and hoped for the unity of the colonies. Charles Carroll of Carrollton signed the Declaration Independence with the strong conviction that political freedom from British rule would bring religious freedom to Maryland and the other colonies.

The Quebec Act of 1774 in Canada brought consternation to some of the American Colonists. Why? Because it restored the French civil laws and freedom of worship to the Catholics of Canada. Fear, bigotry and prejudice resulted. House was divided against house and even parents took issue with their children on the question of being a Whig, Patriot and Rebel against those who termed themselves Loyalists and Tories. During the occupation of Philadelphia by the British, executions took place on the present site of City Hall. It must be admitted that after the British left Philadelphia, the Whigs also executed their enemies on the self-same site of the citadel of William Penn's brotherly love. This was done, of course, on the basis of necessity and the prevailing court martial.

It can easily be understood that it was difficult to be a practical Catholic during the British invasion and occupation of certain cities, since the British considered the "Test Oath" a norm of good morality. William Penn's Philosophy of "live and let live" could not be taught to the bigots of Revolutionary days until the statesman, Thomas Jefferson, after much debate and determination engrafted the principles of religious liberty into the very Constitution of the United States of America. The assistence of Catholic France's military, naval and financial aid to America's cause and the testimony of George Washington concerning the loyalty of Catholics to the new nation gradually broke down the bars of bigotry which were indelibly written from 1693 to 1773 in the obnoxious Test oath which was indispensible for anyone holding office under the Crown and Proprieties. It may be of interest to the reader to glance at the wording of this abdominable document from which even the most callous Catholics would shrink and rightly prefer poverty and obscurity to publicity and vain honor in those perilous days.

"We and each of us do solemnly swear and sincerely profess and testify that in the Sacrament of the Lord's Supper there is no transubstantion of the elements of bread and wine into the Body and Blood of Christ, at or after the consecration thereof by any person whatsoever, and that the invocation or adoration of the Virgin Mary, or any other Saint, and the Sacrifice of the Mass, as they are now used in the Church of Rome, are superstitious and idolatrous." (Stille—Religious Tests in Provincial Pennsylvania p. 30.)

This Test Oath, the reader may remember, was abrogated by the Convention in Philadelphia in May 1787 when the Sixth Article of the Constitution was adopted "that no religious test shall ever be required as a qualification to any office or public trust." The spirit of this Test Oath prevailed during these depressing years of 1777 and 1778 and naturally, even if not openly enforced, it submerged the Catholics as well as Barry in their attempt to assume leadership in the nation's welfare. Catholics were often in a dilemma as to where their loyalty should be placed, especially when they heard that in 1777, William Henry, Duke of Glouchester, and Prince Edward Augustus, the two brothers of King George III of England, paid a visit to Rome and were received with honor by Pope Pius VI. In 1778 the Catholic Relief Act was passed and England was conciliating the clergy of Ireland. These major events in history humiliated the Catholics in America and often divided the Catholics in their allegiance to Washington and his principles of Independence. What was the effect upon Barry? He realized his prerogative of fidelity to Washington and with such independent thinkers as Charles Carrol of Carrolton, he openly proclaimed his allegiance to Washington and his fight for Independence from Britain.

During the evacuation of Philadelphia by the British, the city of Philadelphia was often controlled by many

Americans who feared France as an ally because that
nation was reputedly known to be Catholic. Washington's
friends, such as Barry, DuPortail, Lafayette, Pulaski,
Kociusko, Fitzgerald, FitzSimmons and Charles Carroll
of Carrollton, were feared because they were Catholics.
To live in Philadelphia, which had been named "the
city of Brotherly Love" by William Penn, merited place-
ment on a Role of Honor for a practical Catholic. In spite
of the loyalty and service of Catholics, they were feared
by high-tensioned historians who argued from the defects of a few Catholics that all were incapable of loyalty
to Washington. Barry was one of those Catholics who
elicited the admiration and personal friendship of
Washington who publicly said that he desired the
Catholics of America "to enjoy every temporal and
spiritual felicity."

Barry practised his Catholic Faith and the cause of
Independence he placed in the hands of God and General
Washington. He was suppressed but never depressed! He
never failed to rise to leadership with or without recognition and honor. He wrote very little about himself and
never asked for honor and glory, for he felt that his
personal friendship with Washington proved his fidelity
to the cause of American Independence for which he
planned to live and die.

During this period of extreme depression when
patriotic and God-loving men looked for the worst but
hoped for the best, an amusing but psychologically effective "Trojan Horse" of military strategy was injected
into the city of Philadelphia which was then occupied
by the British troops. On January 5th 1778, when Philadelphia was in despair and the British were celebrating
festivities of many kinds, Washington and Barry had
hope of victory through constant harassment of British
shipping and to the surprise of the British staged a new
form of attack on British ships bringing stores and sup-

plies to America. The manouvere was prophetic of the sub-marine which in later centures wrought devastation on and under the sea. Kegs were loaded with dynamite and sent floating down the Delaware River and when they reached the city of Philadelphia, sentries thought the kegs contained an attacking force of Americans and immediately fired their muskets and volley after volley set the kegs afire and rent the air with explosions. By some historians the affair was termed "the Battle of the Kegs." The result was that some shipping was destroyed but the psychological impact was of major importance because the exploding kegs in passing down stream threw Philadelphia into a panic. The new mode of warfare was helpful for the colonists!

During these two years of extreme depression, what was Jones doing? By order of Congress, Jones was directed to carry out a campaign of harassment of all vessels bearing aid of any kind to the British army or navy and its emissaries in the Revolutionary War. After capturing many vessels laden with food, clothing and the munitions of war, Jones convoyed them to some safe American port for immediate use by the American army and navy. It was on the "Alfred" of which he was Captain that Jones went to Pensacola and covered the Atlantic along the Atlantic Seaboard from north to south. In spite of Jones powerful method of distressing the British the war seemed stalemated and many colonists tiring of warfare even deserted the cause of Washington and went over to the cause of the "Loyalists" or followers of the British plan of liberty.

It is said that Sir William Howe made an offer to Barry to desert Washington and become one of the leaders of the British, to which Barry replied quite tartly: "Not the value and command of the whole British Fleet can lure me from the cause of my country." Dr. Benjamin Rush, the eminent Philadelphia physician, also said of

Barry "America was the object of Barry's patriotism and the theatre of his usefulness in the Revolutionary War which established the independence of the United States."

Jones succeeded well in his harassment campaign for on April 10th 1778 he encountered the British ship "Drake" and victory was conceded to the "Ranger" of which Jones was Captain. During the entire summer and autumn of 1778 Jones sailed the Atlantic ocean and finally on October 19th landed at Brest where from the French nation he received as a gift the "Duc de Doras." This ship he quickly re-named on December 8th after the literary hero of Benjamin Franklin "Bonhomme Richard." This ship became the epic and heroic emblem of victory over the British Fleet at Flamborough Head on September 23rd 1779 and made Jones one of the outstanding heroes of the Revolutionary War. The cruising hours of Jones were well utilized by his insatiable literary talents and thus he left little unsaid or unwritten which he accomplished. He could well repeat the memorable lines of Horace "Exegi Monumentum"—I have raised a monument of my personal glory—the apostrophe of my sole ambition!

Reconnaissance

BARRY	JONES
1777–Feb. 12th–Barry was Senior Commander of the American Navy at the Port of Philadelphia, where he engaged all his time to Naval Defense.	1777–Jan. 14th–Captain Jones replaced of command of "Alfred" by Captain Himman, because of violent dispute over escape of "Glasgow" in a running battle of April 9th 1776.
June 14–Congress adopts the "Striped Flag" which Barry had used as early as 1775 on the "Lexington" while Jones used the "Rattlesnake Flag" on the "Alfred."	Feb. 5th–Jones received an order from Congress to command private expedition against Pensacola and other places with the "Alfred," "Columbus,"

Reconnaissance

BARRY	JONES
Sept. 11th–After the battle of Brandywine, the Liberty Bell was secretly taken out of Philadelphia. It was reported as sunk and hidden in the Delaware River, but truthfully it was hauled to Allentown, Pennsylvania, where it was hidden in the lower walls of Zion's Reformed Church, Church & Hamilton Streets.	"Cabot," "Hampden" and "Providence." Jones was left at liberty to adopt measures which he thought best. Jones went from Boston to Philadelphia.

BARRY

Sept. 20th–British occupy Philadelphia. General Howe enters city and makes an offer to Barry to desert the American Colonists under Washington. Barry's answer was negative. "Not the value of the whole British Fleet can lure me from the cause of my country."

Nov. 16th–Fort Mifflin attacked by British.

Nov. 23rd–Navy Board ordered all boats on Delaware River to move south or north of Market Street to avoid capture by British.

1778–Jan. 5th–"Battle of the Kegs." During the British invasion of Philadelphia, outside the city there was utter despair, while within the city there was "joy unconfined" amongst the British officers and those who had deserted from General Washington. Washington and Barry had faith and plans for their cause of independence and pro-

JONES

1778–Jan. 10th–Jones was ordered to equip the "Ranger" and go to sea for the purpose of distressing the enemy and also for the purpose of convoying American vessels with safety to their destination.

April 10th–Jones sailed from Brest with intentions of striking on the south side of England. Encountered the "Drake" which hoisted the English colors but at the same time the American Stars were displayed aboard the "Ranger." Engagement followed. The commander of the "Drake" fell and victory was declared in favor of the "Ranger."

Summer & Autumn–Jones sailed the Atlantic to harass the British shipping.

Oct. 19th–Jones landed at Brest from the Irish Channel in the "Ranger." Later the "Duc de Doras" given by France to America was re-named "La Bonhomme Richard" as a compliment to the Literary hero of Benjamin Franklin, namely "Poor Richard." The Fleet consisting of "Bonhomme Richard," "Alliance," "Pallas,"

Reconnaissance

BARRY	JONES
posed harassment for British shipping on the Delaware River. Washington prayed in the snows of Valley Forge while Barry filled kegs with explosive powder and floated them down the surface of the river. The shore batteries poured shot and shell into the explosive kegs which naturally threw the British ships into a panic. By writers the affair was called "The Battle of the Kegs" and occurred after the destruction of the "Effingham."	"Vengeance" and "Corfu" under command of Jones for anticipated battle with English Fleet. Jones prepared to meet the British near Flamborough Head.

Jan. 10th–Barry appeared before Congress in York, Pennsylvania, to explain the loss of the "Effingham" and the "Hopkinson Dispute." Barry visited General Washington at Valley Forge.

Jan. 29th–Barry cruises in upper Delaware River to destroy all British shipping.

March 7th–Barry captured "Mermaid" and "Kitty" laden with supplies for British. The "Alert" surrendered to Barry which gave Washington much consolation at Valley Forge.

April–The "Effingham" and "Washington" sunk near Bordentown, N. J., by orders of General Washington, but later raised from the soft bottom of the Delaware River.

Reconnaissance

BARRY	JONES
May 7th–British burn 21 vessels, naval stores and supplies, including Barry's ship the "Effingham" in the upper Delaware.	
May 10th–Marine Committee orders Barry to command the "Raleigh" in Boston Harbor. Barry patrolled the coast from North Carolina to Massachusetts.	
June 18th–British evacuated Philadelphia.	
Sept. 18th–Barry lost "Raleigh" off Seal Island, Penobscot Bay, in battle vs. "Experiment" and "Unicorn" on the rocks of uninhabited Island. Ran the "Raleigh" on the shores to avoid capture and then ordered the ship to be set afire. Barry was praised by the Marine Committee for the battle and defense of the "Raleigh."	

CHAPTER VI

Jones Scores His Greatest Victory
Sept. 23rd 1779

The period of 1779 to 1781 was highlighted by the sea battle and victory of Jones when the "Le Bonhomme Richard" met the British man of war, the "Serapis," off Flamborough Head. Jones received immortal renown for his indomitable courage and excellent seamanship. It is evident from the historical records which are descriptive of that battle on September 23rd 1779 that Captain Jones truthfully knew the poor condition of his ship, but used it with courage and skill to deceive the "Serapis" and its gallant but frustrated Captain Pearson. Jones not only had an inferior ship, but he had to face the problem of released prisoners aboard the "Bonhomme Richard," confused or indifferent officers and the danger of being destroyed by raging fires and the in-take of water which threatened to scuttle the ship. It was only the next morning after the battle that the "Bonhomme Richard" was found to be a limping, worthless and dying hulk.

In telling the story of this important sea-battle, no better words can be found than those of the victor— Captain John Paul Jones! The personal appreciation of the psychological feeling and intellectual strategy of Jones will be found in the following abstract from the official account of Jones as we have found it in "The Life of John Paul Jones" which was compiled and edited by James Otis in the year 1900 from the collection of manuscripts prepared by John Henry Sherburne. Nobody has told the story better than Captain Jones himself in this verbatim record:

Jean Antoine Houdon—Sculptor

JOHN PAUL JONES
1747–1792

BATTLE OFF FLAMBOROUGH HEAD

"On the 21st of September 1779, we saw and chased two sail off Flamborough Head; the "Pallas" chased in the N.E. quarter, while the "Bonhomme Richard," followed by the "Vengeance," chase in the S.W.; the one I chased, a brigantine collier in ballast, belonging to Scarborough, was soon taken, and sunk immediately afterwards, as a fleet then appeared to the southward. This was so late in the day that I could not come up with the fleet before night; at length, however, I got so near one of them as to force her to run ashore between Flamborough Head and the Spurn. Soon after I took another, a brigantine from Holland, belonging to Sunderland, and at daylight the next morning, seeing a fleet steering towards me, I imagined them to be a convoy bound from London for Leith, which had been for some time expected. One of them had a pennant hoisted, and appeared to be a ship of force. They had not, however, courage to come on, but kept back, all except the one which seemed to be armed, and that one also kept to the windward, very near the land, and on the edge of dangerous shoals, where I could not with safety approach. This induced me to make a signal for pilot, and soon afterwards two pilots' boats came off. They informed me that a ship that wore a pennant was an armed merchantman, and that a king's frigate lay there in sight, at anchor, within the Humber, waiting to take under convoy a number of merchant ships bound to the northward. The pilots imagined the "Bonhomme Richard" to be an English ship-of-war, and consequently communicated to me the private signal which they had been required to make. I endeavored by this means to decoy the ships out of the port; but the wind then changing, and with the tide becoming unfavorable for them, the deception had not the desired effect, and they wisely put back. The entrance of the Humber is exceedingly difficult and dangerous, and as the "Pallas" was not in sight I thought it imprudent to remain off Flamborough Head. In the night we saw and chased two ships until three o'clock in the morning, when, being at a very small distance from them, I made the private signal of reconnaissance, which I had given to each captain before I sailed from Groix: one half of the answer only was returned. In this position both sides lay to till daylight, when the ships proved to be the "Alleance" and "Pallas.""

"On the morning of that day, the 23d of September 1779, the brig from Holland not being in sight, we chased a brigantine that appeared laying to, to windward. About noon we saw and chased a large ship that appeared coming round Flamborough Head, from the northward, and at the same time I manned and armed one of the pilot boats to send in pursuit of the brigantine, and which now appeared to be the vessel that I had forced ashore. Soon after this, a fleet of forty-one sail appeared off Flamborough Head bearing N.N.E. This induced me to abandon the single ship which had then anchored in Burlington Bay; I also called back the pilot boat, and hoisted a signal for general chase. When the fleet discovered us bearing down, all the merchant ships crowded sail towards the shore. The two ships-of-war that protected the fleet at the same time steered from the land, and made the disposition for battle. In approaching the enemy, I crowded every possible sail, and made the signal for the line of battle, to which the "Alleance" showed no attention. Earnest as I was for the action, I could not reach the commodore's ship until seven in the evening, being then within pistol shot, when he hailed the "Bonhomme Richard." We answered him by firing a whole broadside.

"The battle, being thus begun, was continued with unremitting fury. Every method was practised on boths sides to gain an advantage, and rake each other; and I must confess that the enemy's ship, being much more manageable than the "Bonhomme Richard," gained thereby several times an advantageous situation, in spite of my best endeavors to prevent it. As I had to deal with an enemy of greatly superior force, I was under the necessity of closing with him, to prevent the advantage which he had over me in point of manoeuvre. It was my intention to lay the "Bonhomme Richard" athwart the enemy's bow; but as that operation required great dexterity in the management of both sails and helm, and some of our braces being shot away, it did not exactly succeed to my wish. The enemy's bowsprit, however, came over the "Bonhomme Richard's" poop by the mizzen-mast, and I made both ships fast together in that situation, which, by the action of the wind on the enemy's sails, forced her stern close to the "Bonhomme Richard's" bow, so that the ships lay square along side of each other, the yards being all entangled, and the cannon of each ship touching the opponent's. When this position took place, it was eight o'clock, previous to which the "Bonhomme

Richard" had received sundry eighteen-pound shots below the water, and leaked very much. My battery of twelve-pounders, on which I had placed my chief dependence, being commanded by Lieutenant Dale and Colonel Weibert, and manned principally with American seamen and French volunteers was entirely silenced and abandoned. As to the six old eighteen-pounders that formed the battery of the lower gundeck, they did no service whatever, exept firing eight shot in all. Two out of three of them burst at the first fire, and killed almost all the men who were stationed to manage them."

"Before this time, too, Colonel de Chamillard, who commanded a party of twenty soldiers on the poop, had abandoned that station after having lost some of his men. I had now only two pieces of cannon (nine-pounders) on the quarter-deck, that were not silenced, and not one of the heavier cannon was fired during the action. The purser, M. Mease, who commanded the guns on the quarter-deck, being dangerously wounded in the head, I was obliged to fill his place, and with great difficulty rallied a few men, and shifted over one of the lee quarter-deck guns, so that we afterwards played three pieces of nine-pounders upon the enemy."

"The tops alone seconded the fire of this little battery, and held out bravely during the whole of the action, especially the maintop, where Lieutenant Stack commanded. I directed the fire of one of the three cannon against the main-mast, with double headed shot, while the other two were exceedingly well served with grape and canister shot, to silence the enemy's musketry and clear the decks, which was at last effected. The enemy were, as I have since understood, on the instant of calling for quarter, when the cowardice or treachery of three of my under-officers induced them to call to the enemy. The English commodore asked me if I demanded quarter, and I having answered him in the most determined negative, they renewed the battle with double fury."

"They were unable to stand the deck; but the fire of their cannon, especially the lower battery, which was entirely formed of ten-pounders, was incessant; both ships were set on fire in various places, and the scene was dreadful beyond the reach of language. To account for the timidity of my three under-officers, I mean, the gunner, the carpenter, and the master at-arms, I must observe that the first two were slightly wounded, and, as the ship had received various shot under water, and one of the pumps being shot away, the carpenter expressed his fears that she would sink, and the other two concluded that she was sinking, which occasioned the gunner to run aft on the poop, without my knowledge, to strike the colors. Fortunately for me, a cannon ball had done that before, by carrying away the ensign-staff; he was therefore reduced to the necessity of sinking, as he supposed, or of calling for quarter, and he preferred the latter."

"All this time the "Bonhomme Richard" had sustained the action alone, and the enemy, though much superior in force, would have been very glad to have got clear, as appears by their own acknowledgments, and by their having let go an anchor the instant that I laid them on board, by which means they would have escaped, had I not made them well fast to the "Bonhomme Richard."

"At last, at half-past nine o'clock, the "Alliance" appeared, and I now thought the battle at an end; but, to my utter astonishment, he discharged a broadside full into the stern of the "Bonhomme Richard." We called to him for God's sake to forbear firing into the "Bonhomme Richard", yet they passed along the off-side of the ship, and continued firing. There was no possibility of his mistaking the enemy's ship for the "Bonhomme Richard," there being the most essential difference in their appearance and construction. Besides, it was then full moonlight, and the sides of "Bonhomme Richard" were all black, while the sides of the prize were all yellow. Yet, for the greater security, I showed the signal of our reconnoissance, by putting out three lanterns, one at the ead, another at the stern, and the third in the middle, in a horizontal line."

"Every tongue cried that he was firing into the wrong ship, but nothing availed; he passed round, firing into the "Bonhomme Richard's" head, stern, and broadside, and by reconnaissance one of his volleys killed several of my best men, and mortally wounded a good officer on the forecastle only. My situation was really deplorable; the "Bonhomme Richard" received various shot under water from the "Alliance," the leak gained on the pumps, and the fire increased much on board both ships."

"Some officers persuaded me to strike, of whose courage and good sense I entertain a high opinion. My treacherous master-at-arms let loose all my prisoners without my knowledge, and my prospects became gloomy indeed. I would not, however, give up the point."

"The enemy's main mast began to shake; their firing decreased fast; ours rather increased, and the British colors were struck, so both Captain Jones and Captain Pearson report."

Jones notices it as very remarkable how well the three light quarter-deck guns were seized during the whole action, and the confusion that ensued when the water was gaining below, the ships alternately catching fire from each other, the "Alliance" firing at the "Bonhomme Richard," and the prisoners set loose.

"He got one of the off guns over soon after the "Alliance" raided the first time, but could never muster strength sufficient to bring over the other." In the clear moonlight, the enemy's mast being painted yellow, the flames of the main shrouds, etc., made the mainmast a distinct mark.

"There was no occasion for a boat or bridge between the two ships. Captain Person stepped on board the "Bonhomme Richard", and delivered up his sword to Captain Jones, who returned it to him, because he had bravely used it. He then heard, and the next morning saw, with astonishment, the inferior force and mangled condition of the "Bonhomme Richard."

"This prize proved to be the British ship-of war "Serapis," a new ship of forty-four guns, built on the most approved construction, with two complete batteries, one of them of eighteen-pounders, and commanded by the brave Commodore Richard Pearson. I had yet two enemies to encounter, far more formidable than the British, I mean fire and water. The "Serapis" was attacked only by the first; but the "Bonhomme Richard" was assailed by both; there was five feet of water in the hold and though it was moderate from the explosion of so much gunpowder, yet the three pumps that remained would with difficulty only keep the water from gaining. The fire broke out in various parts of the ship, in spite of all the water that could be thrown in to quench it, and at length broke out as low as the powder magazine, and within a few inches of the powder."

"In that dilemma, I took out the powder upon deck, ready to be thrown overboard at the last extremity, and it was ten o'clock the next day, the 24th, before the fire was entirely extinguished."

"With respect to the situation of the "Bonhomme Richard" the rudder was cut entirely off, the stern frame and transoms were almost entirely cut away, and the timber by the lower deck, especially from the mainmast towards the

stern, being greatly decayed with age, were mangled beyond
power of description, and a person must have been an eye-
witness to form a just idea of the tremendous scene of carnage,
wreck, and ruin, which everywhere appeared."

"The "Bonhomme Richard" received little damage in
her masts; but was cut entirely to pieces between decks, especially from the mainmast to the stern. In that space, there
was an entire break on both sides, from the gun-deck, almost
to the water's edge; so that towards the end of the action, almost all the shot of the "Serapis" had passed through the
"Bonhomme Richard," without touching. The rudder and
transoms were cut off; and here and there an old rotten timber,
besides the stern-post, was the only support that prevented the
stern from falling down on the gun-room deck. Eight or ten of
the "Bonhomme Richard's" men took away a fine cutter boat,
that had been at the stern of the "Serapis" during the action,
and landed at Scarborough. Some others were much afraid as
to swim on board the "Alliance" after the action."

"AFTER the carpenters, as well as Captain Cottineau
and other men of sense, had well examined and surveyed the
ship (which was not finished before five in the evening), I
found every person to be convinced that it was impossible to
keep the "Bonhomme Richard" afloat so as to reach a port, if
the wind should increase, it being then only a very moderate
breeze. I had but little time to remove my wounded, which was
effected in the course of the night and next morning."

"I was determined to keep the "Bonhomme Richard"
afloat and, if possible, to bring her into port. For that purpose,
the first lieutenant of the "Pallas" continued on board with a
party of men to attend the pumps, with boats in waiting ready
to take them on board, in case the water should gain on them
too fast. The wind augmented in the night, and the next day,
the 25th, so that it was impossible to prevent the good old ship
from sinking. They did not abandon her till after nine o'clock;
the water was then up to the lower deck, and a little after ten I
saw with inexpressible grief, the last glimpse of the "Bonhomme
Richard." No lives were lost with the ship, but it was impossible
to save the stores of any sort whatever. I lost the best part of my
clothes, books, and papers; and several of my officers lost all
their clothes and effects."

"Captain Cottineau engaged the "Countess of Scarborough," and took her, after an hour's action, while the

"Bonhomme Richard" engaged the "Serapis." The "Countess of Scarborough" is an armed ship of twenty six-pounders, and was commanded by a king's officer. In the action, the "Countess of Scarborough" and the "Serapis" were at a considerable distance asunder, and the "Alliance," as I am informed, fired into the "Pallas" and killed some men."

"If it should be asked why the convoy was suffered to escape, I must answer that I was myself in no condition to pursue, and that none of the rest showed any inclination; not even Mu. Ricot, who had held off at a distance to windward during the whole action, and withheld by force the pilot boat with my lieutenant and fifteen men, The Alliance, too, was in a state to pursue the fleet, not having a single man wounded, or a single shot fired at her from the "Serapis", and only three that did execution from the "Countess of Scarborough," at such a distance that one struck in the side, and the other two just touched, and then dropped into the water. The "Alliance" killed one man only on board the "Serapis." As Captain de Cottineau charged himself with manning and securing the prisoners of the "Countess of Scarborough," I think the escape of the Baltic fleet cannot so well be charged to his account."

"I should have mentioned that the main-mast and mizzentop-mast of the "Serapis" fell overboard, soon after the Captain had come on board the 'Bonhomme Richard.' "

"The official loss of the wounded on board the "Serapis," of whom eight had died when it is dated, September 30th, 1779, amounts to 68, besides a few whose names could not be ascertained. Of the dead there is no official return before me. In the roll of the "Bonhomme Richard's" equipage, published in Sherburne's Collections, 42 are returned killed, and 40 wounded. There are, however, but 228 names on this imperfect document, which is without date or vouched; and in which the master, Mr. Cutting Lunt, is called the third lieutenant, Mr. Stacey, acting master, the master, etc. Captain Pearson says, "Our loss in the "Serapis" was very great.""

Jones says in his Journal for the King:

"By a return of the surgeon of the "Serapis," they had an hundred men dangerously wounded on board that ship in the action. Their loss appears to be that number killed. They having taken on board some East India seamen at Copenhagen, over and above their complement, their crew appears to have been four hundred effective men, when the action began. Captain Jones had but three hundred and eighty, good and bad, when he left France. He had manned several prizes, which, with desertions on the coast of Ireland and Scotland, and the absence of the pilot boat, with two officers and sixteen of his best men, reduced him to three hundred and forty, including the disaffected, which were a great majority of the whole, as they were chiefy British, who had enlisted from the prisons of France."

"It may also be observed, the officers and men placed in the gunroom, sixty in number, did not discharge a second shot, nor otherwise assist, and cannot properly be said to have been in the action. To say nothing of the damage done by the Countess of Scarbourgh and the "Alliance," the enemy was superior in cannon, as 576 is to 390, besides a greater superiority of men; and had thirteen feet three inches between her guns; wheras, the guns of the "Bonhomme Richard" were only nine feet six inches asunder."

"Captain Jones took command of the "Serapis," and erected jury-masts. After tossing about to and fro in the North Sea, for ten days, in contrary winds and bad weather, in order to gain the port of Dunkirk, on account of the prisoners, the captains under his command, after sone cabal, bore away for the Texel, and left him to windward, with the choice to follow or proceed. (Captain Jones never had three hours' sleep in the twenty-four, in the whole campaign, from L'Orient to the Texel.) The squadron anchored off the Texel the 3d of October, 1779; and they persisted in working into the port, though the wind was fair for Dunkirk the next morning."

Let this description of the Battle off Scarborough Head be sufficient to justify the many novels, moving pictures and memorials dedicated to the glory of John Paul Jones. Subsequently to this historical event, we find Jones attempting to make settlement of war prizes in Holland and England. Later he received the honor of becoming Chevalier of France with the "Cross of the Order of Military Merit" but was also embroiled in an unpleasant dispute with Captain Landais. Finally he visited Paris for a respite and on February 18th 1781 he returned home to Philadelphia.

Simultaneously in America, Barry became commander of the "Brigantine" on February 15th 1779, and on July 18th he captured the British ship "Harlem" with 14 four-pounders. On November 6th, Barry was placed in command of the "Continental" a 74 gun man of war, which was completed at Portsmouth, N.H., and its name changed to the "America." Barry also entered politics and openly opposed the many injustices perpetrated by the inefficient Marine Committee in the formative years of the American Navy. Barry's work in assisting General Wayne to obtain supplies for General Washington at Valley Forge helped to hold together the struggling Americans, and his vital concern in obtaining forage, food, clothing and supplies for Colonel Stephen Moylan of the Pennsylvania Dragoons in his dire distress manifested his deepest concern for the unity of purpose of the militant forces both on land and sea.

Reconnaissance

BARRY	JONES
1779–Feb. 15th–Barry commander of the "Brigantine" changed name to the "Delaware" and carried 10 guns and 45 men when commissioned.	1779–June 14th–Jones employed to convoy a fleet to Bordeaux and other ports in the Bay of Biscay.
July 18th–Barry captures the "Harlem" with 14 four-pounders and 85 men of the British fleet. The British ship "Confederacy" attempts to take over the ship under Barry's command but failed.	July 2nd–"Bonhomme Richard" found in need of repairs and declared fit only for extemporary service.
	Aug. 14th–Jones sailed with his squadron from Groix.
Nov. 6th–Barry was ordered to the new "Continental" a 74 gun ship which was later named the "America."	Sept. 23rd–Jones wins major sea-battle off Flamborough, the "Bonhomme Richard" conquers the British "Serapis." Captain Pearson delivered his sword to Jones. "Serapis" taken

Reconnaissance

BARRY	JONES
Dec. 12th–Barry in Philadelphia complained about the Marine Committee and its manifold injustices by ignorant judges and public scandal.	as prize with 44 guns and 2 complete batteries, 42 men. In the battle, when Jones was asked to surrender, he replied "Never! I have not yet begun to fight."
	Oct. 3rd–The squardon under Jones command anchored off Trexel.
	Oct. 15th–Letter from Benjamin Franklin to Jones in answer to Jones report of the engagement with the "Serapis" 504 prisoners returned to France. Dissatisfaction with Captain Landais.
	Oct. 28th–Jones wrote to Lafayette that he never meant to ask for a reward for his service to France or America.
	Dec. 15th–Plans made to give Jones a French commission, which Jones regarded as an insult.

CHAPTER VII

Barry's Battle and Triumph
May 28th 1781

The melancholy picture of the early months of 1781 were not inspiring to the army and navy of Washington. The people were divided into groups, one which sought peace at any price and the other which fought and made many sacrifices for independence from England. The litany of sorrow which swept over the colonies consisted of these important historical facts:

1—Charleston was occupied by the British.

2—South Carolina was ravaged by the British.

3—Georgia was crushed by British occupational forces.

4—Cornwallis was succeeding in his plans to conquer the South.

5—General Benedict Arnold became a Traitor.

6—Mutiny existed in Pennsylvania, New Jersey and Connecticut.

7—Mutiny occurred on the American ships for lack of pay.

8—Continental Money depreciated in value.

9—Washington's forces were starving and cold at West Point.

10—Lafayette paid his troops in Virginia with his own money.

11—New York City was occupied by the British.

12—Many desertions occurred in the army and navy.

13—The authority of Congress was at low ebb.

14—Instead of being united, the Colonies were divided.

15—High taxes prevailed.

16—Discontent, gloom and chaos reigned supreme.

If you can properly synchronize all these ingredients of a broken-hearted people, then you will have the correct picture of the proposed United States of America in 1781. Washington himself wrote to Laurens in France "we are at the end of our tether and now or never our deliverance must come."

There was need of an American Victory to give courage to the fighting forces for Independence from British rule. There was positive need of funds to sustain Washington and his loyal followers. How did Barry and Jones fit into this chaotic state of affairs? Barry was out on the open seas engaged in the harassment of British shipping on the Atlantic while Jones was in Philadelphia seeking from Congress honors for his service and higher promotion as Admiral and Head of the Navy. Jones was properly accredited for his sea-victories but never made Admiral nor placed in higher authority over Barry.

At this critical moment of discouragement in 1781, Barry actually captured four important vessels of the British, namely, the "Mars," "Minerva," Atalanta" and "Trepassy." The last two of these vessels were overtaken in battle which added lustre to Barry's record of seamanship. The story of this battle which occured on May 28th 1781 between Barry's vessel the "Alliance" against the "Atalanta" and "Trepassy" of England, may be summarized in the words of Barry's records as found in the works of the historian Martin Griffin.

We shall first quote the record made by Kessler:

"May 28th. Towards evening discovered two sail on the weather bow standing for us and which after coming near enough to be kept in sight hauled to wind and stood on our course. Towards day it became quite calm. AFTER it became light it appeared that they were an armed ship and brig—about a league distant. At sunrise they hoisted the English colors and beat drums. At the same time the American colors were displayed by the "Alliance." By little puffs of wind we were enabled to get within short hailing distance. At eleven o'clock Captain Barry hailed the ship, and was answered that she was the "Atalanta" ship of war belonging to His Britannic Majesty, commanded by Captain (Sampson) Edwards. Captain Barry then told Captain Edwards that we were the Continental frigate "Alliance" and commanded by John Barry and advised him to haul down his colors. Captain Edwards answered: 'Thank you sir. Perhaps I may after a trial.' The firing then began, but unfortunately there was not wind enough for our steerage way, and they being lighter vessels by using sweeps got and kept athwart our stern and on our quarters so that we could not bring one-half our guns nay, oft time, only one gun, out astern to bear on them, and thus laying like a log the greatest part of the time."

"About two o'clock Captain Barry received a wound by a grape shot in the shoulder. He remained, however, on the quarter deck until by the much loss of blood he was obliged to be helped to the cock-pit. Some time after our colors were shot away and it so happened that at the same time such guns as would bear on them had been fired and were then loading and which led the enemy to think we had struck the colors and manned their shrouds and gave three cheers by that time the colors were hoisted by a mizin brail and our firing again began. A quartermaster went to the wheel in place of one just killed there. At the moment a small breeze of wind happening a broadside was brought to bear and fired on the ship and then one on the brig, when they struck the ircolors at three o'clock."

"I was ordered to fetch the Captain on board. Finding the Captain of brig killed, the Captain of the ship was brought. On his entrance on board the First Lieutenant received him and to whom he offered his sword but which was not received and he was informed that he was not the Captain; that Captain Barry was wounded and in the cabin, to whom he was conducted. On his entrance into the cabin (Captain Barry then seated in an easy chair, his wounds dressed) he advanced to Captain Barry and presented his sword and which Captain

Barry received, then returned to Captain Edwards, saying: I
return it to you, sir. You have merited it and your King ought
to give you a better ship. Here is my cabin at your service. Use
it as if your own. He then ordered the Lieutenant of the brig
to be brought, after which it was agreed that the crew of the
ship, together with the prisoners on board the "Alliance,"
should all be put on board of the brig (called the "Trepassy"
also a King's vessel of 16 guns) and sent as cartel to Halifax,
but Captain Edwards and the Lieutenant of the "Trepassy"
he kept as hostages for the return of the brig with Americans
in return for the 250 British sent. It being, however, too late
in the day to effect the removal, a prize master and crew were
sent on board each and ordered to keep close by us all night.
Captain Edwards and the Lieutenant requested to address
their people and excite then to orderly behavior during the
night, which they did from the quarter-deck of the "Alliance"
and had the desired effect. The next morning the cannon of
the brig were hove overboard and after the arms and ammunition was taken from her, the prisoners were put on board and
she departed for Halifax and the "Alliance" made all sail for
Boston, leaving the prize ship to follow on account of Captain
Barry's wound. It was said, that some time after Captain
Barry had received his wound and left the deck, Lieut. H.
went into the cockpit to Captain Barry and represented that as
the rigging of the ship was very much cut and the ship otherwise much damaged and many men killed and wounded and
considering also the disadvantages we labored under for want
of wind: 'Whether the colors should be struck.' Captain
Barry passionately answered: 'No, sir; and if the ship cannot
be fought without me I will be brought on deck'. The officer
immediately returned to deck and Captain Barry, after being
dressed in haste, was on his way to the deck when the enemy
struck."

"Captain Edwards said they were very confident that they
would subdue the "Alliance." This might appear to be claiming to themselves a superior share of courage and a want on
the part of the "Alliance," if nothing but the disproportion of
number of guns and weight of metal were taken in view; but
when the disadvantages under which the "Alliance" labored
are considered, it will appear they had much reason to flatter
themselves with success and the more so had they known all
those disadvantages; 1st, of the "Alliance's" usual comple-

ment of crew say 280—three prizes had been manned—and of 50 on the Doctor's list, there could not be procured men sufficiently able to sit between decks to hand powder from the magazine, and those who had a mutinous dispostion formed part of the remainder; besides, more than 100 prisoners to take care of and who felt themselves under the lash for their cowardly conduct, and about all the total calm which prevailed until the close of the action. The loss on board was 11 killed and 24 wounded." "I was slightly wounded in the Leg," says Kessler in a later record."

The commission of Captain Edwards surrendered to Captain Barry is now in possession of Captain John S. Barnes, of New York. It is Dated St. John's 13th 1780.

Kessler continues: "June 6th, 1781. The "Alliance" arrived at Boston and Cap'n Barry was immediately landed, and as his wound was considered in a Dangerous state he despatched me express to Philadelphia for Mrs. Barry."

"The "Alliance" was so much shattered in her masts, sails and rigging that a new fore and main mast and a thorough overhauling and repair was necessary, which required much time."

In corroboration of the above quoted "Kessler's Record," we append the Captain Barry's Report of his voyage to France and return to Boston, which is dated June 6th, 1781 as copied by Martin Griffin from the Government Archives in Washington, D.C. and found in his book "Commodore John Barry"—1903.

"Alliance," Frigate, Boston Harbor
June 6th, 1781

To the Board of Admiralty
Gentlemen:

I have the pleasure to inform you of my arrival in Boston after a passage of sixty-nine days from Port L'Orient, at which I arrived, after capturing a small privateer of ten guns and thirty nine men and retaking her prize "Venician." The latter I relieved but the former I took with me where I sold her and distributed the money amongst my officers and crew which pleased them very much as it was more than they had ever received from the "Alliance" before.

"On my arrival at L'Orient I was left destitute of any person to consult with, as Laurens soon left me, however I soon found there was a Ship called the "Marquis de la La-fayette" loading with Continental Stores mounting Twenty-six eight-pounders and fourteen Six-pounder whom I was in-formed was ordered to join the Fleet at Brest to go with them to America. In that case I was determined to Clear the Ship and to comply with my orders to Cruize, but finding the Cap-tain dilatory and loosing his Convoy from L'Orient to Brest and from thence to America I tho't it my duty to Convoy her safe to Philadelphia if possible, I then gave him orders to get himself in readiness while I with my officers did everything in our power to get the "Alliance" in the best order possible, as soon as he was ready we sailed on the 30th day of March from L'Orient with a fair wind."

"On the next day we discovered on board a conspiracy, the ring leaders we confined and have brought them in here in irons. Unhappily for us we had no seaman on board but disaffected ones, and but few of them, I believe a Ship never put to sea in a worse Condition as to seamen."

"On the 2d April we fell in with the Privateer "Mars" of twenty twelve-pounders, two sixes and One hundred and twelve Men, and Privateer Minerva of ten guns and fifty-five men (after taking out her Prisoners) we put a prize Master and a Number of men on board; the latter the "Marquis" manned both of which I ordered for Philadelphia, One of which has since arrived here. The other I suppose went to France."

"We had Continual Gales of Wind on our Passage. One in particular in the Latitude of 40-3 and Longitude of 36. We first split our Fore Topsail and then handed it. About 7 o'clock in the Morning on the 25th April (the "Marquis" close by us, we split our Fore Topsail and then handed it, and soon after our Fore stay sail which deprived us of any head Sail, the "Marquis" being then under her Fore sail she soon shott ahead of us out of sight, and to our great Mortification we could never see her afterwards altho' we did all our en-deavors, standing backwards and forewards looking after her."

"On the 2d May in Lattitude 41d 37m N and Longitude 43. We fell in with a Brig "Snow" loaded with Sugars from

Jamaica which we Captured, and in Case of Separation were ordered for Philadelphia, which was the Case a Short time after wards in a hard Gale of Wind."

"On the 16th May in Lattde 38m 57N and Longd. 53—in a Severe Gale of Wind attended with thunder and lightning One of which Claps cut our Main Top Mast in two and knocked down twelve or fifteen men on deck some of which it burnt some of their Skin off but I thank God all of them have done well since."

"I forgot to mention that in one of the Gales we discovered the Fore Mast very badly Sprung we immediately fixed it in the best manner possible which rendered us incapable of Carrying much Sail."

"On the 19th May in Lattd. 38d. N and 55 of Longitude we fell in with two Ships, we took them to be homeward bound Merchantmen, but being so poorly manned we were not in a Condition to take them, therefore did not hail them.

"On the 28th May in Ltt'd 40d—34m N and Longitude 63.1—we fell in with two of his Britannic Majesty's Sloops of War the "Attalanta" & "Trepassy," the former commanded by Captain Edwards, the Latter by Captain Smith that was killed in the Engagement who bore down upon us and after a Smart Action we had five Men killed and twenty-two wounded, three of which has died of their wounds since. I am amongst the wounded the Occasion of my wound was a Large Grape Shott which lodged in my left Shoulder, which was soon after cut out by the Surgeon, I am flattered by him that I shall be fit for duty before the Ship will be ready to Sail and I am of the same opinion as the Ship is shattered in a most shocking manner and wants new Masts, Yards, Sail and Rigging,—Soon after the Sloops of War struck I tho't it most Prudent to throw all the "Trepassey's" Guns overboard and take away all her military store and to fit her out as a Cartel and to send all the Prisoners I had on board with them I had that day taken, for Newfoundland, which the Captain of the "Atalanta", assured me should be regularly exchanged, only keeping on board the Captain of the "Atalanta," the Purser, Doctor and Wounded; and the Senior officer of the "Trepassy" with a few others. As the "Atalanta" was the largest Vessel and Copper bottomed I got Jury Masts upon her (she being dismasted in the action) and ordered her to Boston which I tho't the Nearest and safest Port, we being at that time in a Shattered Condition very foul and hardly Men enough to work our Ship I tho't most prudent to make the nearest Port we could, hoping it will meet with Your Honors' approbation; I cannot help mentioning ONE particular circumstance respecting a Quantity of Copper and Nails fitt for Sheathing Ships which has laid in the hands of the Continental Agents and Navy Board for these three Years. Whether It was sent for any other purpose or not I cannot tell, but I am sure it is fit for nothing else, It will not cost so much to it on the Ship as it will to Clean her, if you would order the "Alliance" to be sheathed with it you may keep her the whole War, if not you may be assured that whenever she is Catched at sea foul that you will lose her.

"I have given you a Short Sketch of my Operations from the time I sailed from Boston until the present time which I hope will meet with your approbation, Your Attention particular to Sheathing the Ship with Copper will render an essential Service to the Country and Much oblige.

"Your Most obedient and very
"humble serv't

John Barry

"P.S. I hear the "Snow" with Sugars is in a Safe Port to the Eastward & expect the "Atalanta" in every hour.

(Endorsed) "Captain Barry's Letter of 6 June, 1781, to the Board of Admralty—1 Enclosure."

The "SNOW" was "a vessel with two masts resembling the main and foremast of a ship, and a third small mast just abaft the mainmast carrying a sail similar to a ship's mizzen."

Captain Barry's report to the Naval Board relates events of the voyage to France and return to America. It reads:

"To the Honorable Naval Board Eastern Department, June 6th (1781)."

"GENTLEMEN: For sufficient reasons as per Log we were obliged to cut our Cable to get under way from Nantasket road on the 11th of February. Nothing remarkable to the 16th instant when we fell in within the Night Large fields of ice and Blowing very hard, we continued in the ice about

12 hours the Ship Laboring very much we recd Considerable damage in Latitude 42°03'N; Longd 55°03' west on the 4th day of March 47°31' D.R. Longd 4°27' we fell in with and took a Privateer Schooner from Glasgow Mounting 10 Carriage Guns, called the "ALERT" Francis Russel Cammander, sent Mr. Nichs Garden Prize Master, who arrived safe in L'Orient, Friday the 9th of March."

"Saturday we come to Anchor at Port Louis Friday the 30th of March we slipt our Moorings and got under way in Company with the ship Marquis de La Fayette 31st of do. We found out a number of men who had conspired to take the ship from us to Carry her into England and punished them in such a manner as made them Confess the Crime laid to their Charge Monday 2nd of April we fell in with and took 2 Privateer Brigs from Guernsey one was the "Mars" of 20 12-lb. and 2 6-lb. and 12 4-pound Cohorns Jno. Prero Commander, the other was the "Minerva" of 8 4-pound cannon and 55 men John Lecost Commander the first Brig Manned by us Lieut. Fletcher Prize Master the "Minerva "manned by the Marquis 19th Instant Lost Sight of both Brigs 26th Instant Lost Sight of the Marquis in a Gale of Wind and May the 2nd & 3d took a Brig and the "Snow" from Jamaica bound to Bristol in the Lattd. of 41°30' Longd. 41°30' West Laden with Sugar."

"Thursday the 12th of May Lost Sight of the Brig and Snow in the Lattd. of 39°81' Longd. 55°81' West, heavy Gales of Wind Thunder and Lightning. 17th of May Lightning Struck our Main Top Mast and Shivered him from Cross trees to CAP sprung our Foremast very badly the Lightning burnt one man and knocked down several, in the Lattd. 38°57' Longd. 52°46' West."

"29th of May fell in with Two English sloops of War one a Ship Mounting 16 Carriage Guns and 120 men Capt. Edwards the other a brig of 14 carriage guns AND 60 or 70 men Capt. Smith, the Ship called "Atalanta" the Brig called the "Trepassey" they engaged us with Pistol shott 3 hours when they struck to us, we were very much Shattered in our Riging Spars, and Sail no part of our ship escaped the Fury of their Shott We had 4 men killed and 18 or 20 wounded Among the dangerous wounded was Mr. Prichard, who was shot with a 6 pound shot, him with some more has since died of their wounds, the Ship and Brig in a very shattered condition the ships main mast went over the side the next morning, the ship had 5 men killed and 15 wounded, by their account, the Brig

had 6 men killed the Capt. included, and 12 or 15 wou
fitted out the brig as a Cartel as soon as possible and ho
guns overboard sent between 2 or 300 men on board an
patched her the 31st of May, 1781, Latt. 41°10′ Long.
June 1st parted Company with the "Atalanta" Bou
Boston, Lieut. Welsh on board of her."

"GENTLEMEN for more particulars you will ple
have recourse to the Log Book. 'N.B. Lattd 45°06′ Long
West when we took the 2 Privateer Brigs.' "

More than a month later Captain Barry repor
the Board of Admiralty:

Boston July 25

"GENTS: It is with pleasure that I acquaint your
that I am allmost recovered of my wound and I hope i
4 days to be able to attend my duty for I find my presenc
requisite there being only one Liet. and the Master on
both of them good officers. Captn. Hacker and several
left the ship by permission from the Hon'ble Navy Boar
ing my illness. However I am confident these places
well filled. the master John Buckley have being in th
ever since she was launched he acted as second Liet. fr
11 of July 1779 till he arrived in Boston last year. He
an attachment to the service and his views different from
others he resumed the office of master when I took the
and in that Station behaved as a good and faithful offic
"The ship having but one Liet. on board and non
at present but one. Who is a very young man and
opinion not fit to Com'd men like Buckley but he may
a tolerable 3 Liet. Mr. Buckley has made application to
his friend to use my interest to get him appointed a Lieu
on board the Ship. If my assuring the Hon'ble the Adm
that he was the best Officer I had in the last ship cruize
of any service to him I can on my honor declare it.
your Honors think proper to grant him a Commission
dating from his being appointed an Acting Liet. will
oblige."

Gents. Your Most Obedient
and very Hum'le Ser't

"John Barry"

Captain James Nicholson, writing to Captain
y from Philadelphia, June 24th, 1781, congratulated
upon his safe arrival and his success. He related in
l the endeavor of Chevalier John Paul Jones by per-
l application among the members of Congress to
·e for himself recognition as head of the NAVY.
Nicholson related the measure of success Jones was
·ing and how he thwarted the consummation of the
·ct.

'Your arrival and success came opportunely and I did
il to make use of it. I mean out doors in presence of Cap.
and some of his advocate members by observing that
ad acquitted yourself well, which they acknowledged. I
hem they could not do less than make you an admiral
l had not a sentence of reply. It irritated the Chevalier so
that he was obliged to decamp."

Whatever methods or persuasion Captain John
Jones was using to have himself ranked as "head of
Navy" it seens probably that while Capt. Nicholson
thwarting the endeavor of Jones and expressing
ration of and to Capt. Barry, that he was also look-
o his own recognition. The List of Officers of the
· at his time reads:

. James Nicholson, Commission 10th October, 1776,
ander of "Trumbull."
. John Barry 10th October, 1776, "Alliance."

·et Captain Barry was in active service as com-
er of the "Alliance," the finest ship of the Navy,
he only frigate that escaped capture or destruction
g the war. (Report to Admiralty—Commodore
Barry—Griffin—1903)

CHAPTER VIII

Six Million Catholic Dollars
June 1st 1781

Poverty, distress and defeat haunted the army and navy of Washington throughout the entire Revolutionary War. The picture of Washington at Valley Forge upon his knees in the snow bound forest is a true symbol of our American faith in a provident God before and after Independence was secured. The fighting forces on land and sea were always martyrs in the cause of liberty!

In many instances of administration, the financial means were not available to purchase munitions, clothing and provisions for the service men, and in some cases the individuals in charge of purchasing the necessities of war were incompetent and quarrelsome. Much trouble was experienced in the construction of war vessels for the navy while the quartermasters' warehouses were poorly staffed and the existent forts were miserably equipped and supplied. There was much nepotism and petty politics in the appointments and many business deals with munition manufacturers. Historians admit the favoritism shown in the appointment of captaincies to Continental war vessels but oft times they hesitate to mention the influence of free-masonry in those days of peril. The conspiracy of silence prevails and often it is only through the efforts of such historians as Mrs. Reginald deKoven that the truth is revealed. Augustus C. Buell's imaginative book entitled "Paul Jones— Founder of the American Navy" is used by many authors to promote inspiration to young Americans, but when untruth is used, we only weaken our patriotism and promote disloyalty to America.

(76)

In our study of American history, we discover that not everybody was with General Washington. He had his critics and his enemies, however, the real patriots stood by Washington and fought and prayed with him for independence. The gruesomeness of war was not alone found in the actual killing or wounding of those engaged in battle. The court martials and the subsequent imprisonment or executions were most depressing. In Philadelphia, the present open area within the perimeter of City Hall, was the scene of many executions by the British army during its occupation of the city and also by the Continental Army for its maintenance of law and order. The condemned seamen were oft times executed aboard certain ships at anchor in the Delaware River. These sorrows of war were part and parcel of the American Revolution.

One of the outstanding defections from Washington's army was that of General Benedict Arnold, a native of Connecticut, who through dissatisfaction with military regulations attempted to betray the fortifications of West Point which contained a large consignment of arms and stores which he had planned to turn over to the British. His plan failed through the capture of Major John Andre, Adjutant general in the British army, who was caught in disguise within the American lines and hung as a spy on October 2nd 1780. General Arnold escaped to the British lines but later went to England where he died in disgrace. Other defections and betrayals occurred but such Catholics as Barry, Carroll, Fitzgerald, FitzSimmons, Moylan and the well known French Generals Lafayette, Du Portail, Luzerne, LaRouerie and Rochambeau remained loyal to Washington. The German General DeKalb and the Spanish De Mirales—also fought under the orders of General Washington. Through the influence of a Catholic nation, America obtained not only such gift ships as the "Duc de Doras" which was renamed

the "Bonhomme Richard," but from the individual
zens of Catholic France through its Bishops the su
$6,000,000.00 was given to King Louis XVI for the n
of Washington and his struggling fighters for indep
ence from England.

The story of the financial aid given to Am
may be interesting since little or nothing has ever
publicised about the same. The safe transportation o
large sum of money was assigned to Captain Barry o
ship and brought to the depleted treasury of the col
for the starving and ragged soldiers and sailors as w
their suffering families. Without these funds the cau
America would have been in jeopardy and possibly
against the wealth and increased fighting force of Br
and its hired emissaries from other countries.

In an address by Thomas Dwight of Harvard
versity in Faneuil Hall, Boston in January 1907
lamented the fact that silence prevailed concerning
Gift to America by the French Clergy. In Am
meagre records of the affair were found but proof o
Catholic gratuity was found in the "Minutes of the Ge
Assembly of the Canons Regular of St. Augustine (Gr
Augustins) in the year 1780." After a visit to the Nati
Library of Paris the necessary records for the follo
transcript were found.

"Without the aid given by France, the cause of Engl
revolted colonies was a hopeless one for that time at least
without the timely aid given by the Church to the F
monarchy, the government might not have been able to
tinue the war to a successful issue. This episode, not kno
or ignored by historians, is well worth recording. It is re
here in the very language of the official record.
"By royal decree, October 30th 1779, the re
quinquennial Assembly of the French Clergy was call
meet on Monday, May 20th of the following year (1
The first meeting was held on the date assigned, at wh
committee on credentials was appointed. The Assembly

ɔf two delegates from each of the sixteen (16) ecclesias-
rovinces, one for the hierarchy and one for the lower
"

n June 8th 1780 the subject with which we are here
ned was broached. The letter from the King of France
ad and contained in part the following petition:
His Majesty, having what he had reasons to expect from
evotedness to his interests and glory, and what in the
t circumstances the needs of the State demand, feels
ced that nothing would better comply with his wishes
he request he has commanded us to make of you of a
ary free gift of thirty million of Livres ($6,000,000.00)"
·lics and American Revolution Martin Griffin 1909).

The historian Griffin says that "the grant was really
than that at first appears; the Church had to raise
oney by the sale of bonds on the security of its
"

arry transported this munificent gift of the Catholics
nce safely to America. He left Brest on June 1st
nd arrived in Boston harbor on August 25th 1781.
iip which he used was the "Resolute" which was
also with clothing and munitions in addition to
resaid six million dollars. The story of the transfer
funds from Boston to other points in ox-carts and
means of conveyance is interesting but the main
: of the gift was that it moved Washington's troops
ktown, Virginia, by paying the army one month's
specie and provided supplies for the starving
y and naval forces of America. Congress had no
to obtain money or supplies until the arrival of the
Catholic funds.

While General Benedict Arnold, the traitor, was
g Virginia, he was succeeded by General Corn-
who concentrated his forces in the area of York-
Washington in the meantime pretended to move
s New York City, but finally assembled on Septem-
h 1781, the entire Continental army and its allies

before Yorktown. Batteries opened upon the city and the French vessels in the harbor fired upon the same objective. Two redoubts were carried; one by the Americans and the other by the French. The patriots slept in the air that their allies might use the tents. When breaches were made in the walls, Cornwallis capitulated on October 19th 1781. The victorious troops of Washington were drawn up for the surrender, but the haughty Cornwallis feigned illness and assigned another general to make the formal surrender of his sword. The victory of Yorktown ended the war and gave confidence to all who has assisted Washington in his fight for Independence. Washington gave due credit to the Catholics of France for their financial aid in the worst crisis of the war.

Reconnaissance

BARRY	JONES
1780–Jan. 1st–Barry ordered to complete the construction of "America" which was still under construction in Portsmouth, N. Hampshire.	1780–Jan. 16th–Jones left Texal and went to Corogne, Spain, where he was given reception.
June 1st–Barry placed in full command of the "America" as completed.	June 13th–Captain Landais attempts to command the "Ariel."
	June 21st–Jones arrives at L'Orient, France.
June 8th–King Louis XVI of France requests of French Catholics the sum of six million dollars as a gift to American Independence.	June 28th–Jones received from King of France honored title of "Chevalier" and "Cross of the Order of Military Merit." Visit to Versailles for honors of French Society.
Sept 21st–General Arnold harboring hatred for Washington because of military reprimand, turns traitor and plans to hand over West Point to the British. Escaped to England.	Dec. 18th–Jones leaves France on "Ariel" and enroute met the British frigate "Triumph."
Oct. 2nd–Major John Andre	1781–Feb. 19th–Jones arrives in Philadelphia.

Reconnaissance

BARRY	JONES
hung as spy for his participation in proposed surrender of West Point to British.	March 28th–Board of Admiralty praises Jones for his work.
1781–Feb. 2nd–Barry sailed for France and on this voyage captured the "Alert" and a Venetian boat "La Bouvier Campagnia" which he returned to Venice but kept the "Alert" and brought it to L'Orient where the crew was imprisoned.	April 14th–Congress thanks Jones for his service.

May 15th–Letter of praise to Jones from President Washington. |
| March 29th–"Alliance" left L'Orient for America.

March 31st–Mutiny aboard the "Alliance".
Convoyed "Marquis de Lafayette" loaded with clothing for United States.
April 2nd–Barry captures after battle two ships, namely "Minerva" and the "Mars."
May 2nd–Barry captures British Brig loaded with sugar from Jamaica for London, which he ordered to Boston. | May 28th–Jones addressed Congress and claimed that he was entitled to rank before all persons who did not enter into the sea-service of the continent as early as himself. Jones asked for the rank of "Rear-Admiral" but Congress did not acquiesce because of opposition to same. Higher ranks than that of Captain were not created by Congress until 1862. |
| May 28th–Barry in battle with British ships "Atalanta" and "Trepassy" which were taken over by Barry, namely the "Charlestown" and the "Vulture." In the battle Barry was wounded on the "Alliance" to which Captain Edward of the British "Atalanta" was brought and surrendered his sword to Barry. Barry returned the sword and said: "I return it to you; you have merited it. Your King ought to give you a better | June 23rd–Jones appointed by Congress to command the "America" as Captain.

June 26th–Jones made personal appeal to be made "Head of the Navy."

Aug. 31st–Jones arrived at Portsmouth but found the "America" still unfinished.

Sept. 3rd–Congress decides to give France "America" for loss of "Magnifique."

Oct. 15th–Lafayette writes letlet to Jones concerning attempt to destroy the "America" and |

BARRY

ship. Here is my cabin at your service. Use it as your own."

June 1st–Barry sailed on "Resolute" from Brest, France with $6,000,000.00 gift from Catholic Clergy and People to America.
June 26th–Barry officially in command of the "Alliance"— best ship in the Navy. Jones placed in command of "America" at Portsmouth N. H., with prizes captured by Barry.
July 25th–Barry takes Lafayette to France. The American Navy consisted of only two operable ships under Barry, namely, the "Alliance" and the "Deane."
Sept. 28th.–Washington assembled army before Yorktown with French fleet in harbor for attack upon General Cornwallis.
Oct. 19th–Cornwallis surrenders.
Nov. 21st–Barry ordered to take Lafayette and others to France.
Dec. 23rd–Barry in command of "Alliance" sails from Boston with Lafayette, DuPortail, Noalles, Garvia and LaCombe for France.

1782–Jan. 18th–Barry in port at L'Orient.

March 16th–Sails on "Alliance" from L'Orient for America.

May 10th–"Alliance" was chased by British ship "Chatham" but was not captured. Barry ran "Alliance" at 15

JONES

Jones asks for a special guard for the ship.

Oct. 19th–News of Yorktown Victory arrives while "America" is still in process of completion.

Nov. 5th–Jones launched "America" and turned it over to Chevalier de Martique who formerly commanded the "Magnifique" lost in Boston Harbor.

Dec. 24th–Jones repaired to Boston and sailed with French fleet under Count d'Estang on projected expedition against Jamaica. Congress granted him permission "to acquire improvement in the line of his profession" as Jones requested.

1782–Jones with French Fleet in Atlantic to Spain and South America.

Aboard the "Triomphante," crowded with army of Rochambeau under command of Baron de Viomenil to various ports on voyage.

BARRY

knots per hour and ran down British sloop "Speedwell."

May 23rd–"Alliance" arrived in New London from which place Barry wrote to friends in Philadelphia "I serve the country for nothing."

August 9th–Barry captures the "Polly"

August 19th–Barry landed in the Bermudas St. George's Harbor and then proceeded to New London, Newfoundland and Halifax. Captured the British "Hawk" and "Fortune."

Sept. 8th–Captured "Nantucket Brig." The "Ramilie" foundered in a gale and fleet scattered from Jamaica.

Sept. 24th–Captured British ships "Kingston," "Commerce," "Brittania" and the "Anna."

Oct. 9th–Barry in Bordeaux, France.

Oct. 18th–Report of Cruise made to Congress.

Nov. 30th–Articles of Peace signed.

Dec. 5th–King George III of England ordered end of offensive war with colonies.

Dec. 9th–Barry sailed for Portu Santo.

Dec. 10th–In Port of Island of Madeira with destination to Havana.

JONES

CHAPTER IX

Barry Wins Last Sea Battle
March 10th 1783

The cessation of hostilities does not always immediately precede the signing of a peace treaty, nor does the formal surrender of military forces bring about immediate peace. This will be especially noted in the Revolutionary War. Although General Cornwallis surrendered at Yorktown on October 19th 1781; the Provincial Articles of Peace were signed in Paris on November 30th 1781; the ratification of the same occurred on February 3rd 1783; and the Treaty of Peace arrived in Philadelphia on February 11th 1783; nevertheless, Congress did not order the cessation of hostilities until April 11th 1783 and Washington formally announced the Close of the War on April 19th 1783.

Within this period of time required for the formal settlement of the Revolutionary War, the final sea-battle occurred on March 10th 1783. The engagement took place between the British "Sybille" under command of Captain Vashon and the "Alliance" under Barry's command. The reason for the unexpected encounter can be explained but never condoned as justifiable. The complete strategy and manoeuvre on the part of Barry who was on the defensive were described and praised by his enemy Captain Vashon, who confessed that never before had he received "such a drubbing" and never before saw a ship so ably fought as the "Alliance" under Barry's orders. "The coolness and intrepidity, no less than the skill and fertility in expedients, which Barry displayed on the occasion are described in naval annals as truly wonderful; every quality of a great naval com-

mander was brought out with extraordinary brilliancy."
The "Alliance" fought the last battle of the Revolution
and also saved the specie from Havana in the "Duc de
Lauzun" which funds were used to found the Bank of
North America in Philadelphia.

Some historians assume that the attack of the
"Sybille" upon the "Alliance" was solely an act of
piracy to capture the gold specie upon the American
Ships. The value of the money was estimated at between
one and two hundred thousand dollars and a valuable
cargo was also involved which the British heard Barry
was to transfer from Havana to the United States. Since
the reader of this book may desire to compare the quality
and intensity of Jones' sea battle with the sea-battles of
Barry, we shall use the words of Barry himself to describe
this last sea-battle of the Revolution.

Last Battle 1783

The following is Capt. Barry's report of the Last
Battle of the Revolution, namely between the "Alliance"
and the "Sybille." The quotation is taken from Martin
Griffin's "Commodore John Barry"—1903.

On board the "Alliance," Rhode Island Harbour, March
20, 1783.

Sir:
I have the pleasure to Inform you that on the 6th of
March, 1783 I sailed from the Havana in company with
Capt. Greene with the Duke de Luzerne after being Embargo'd
for 20 days, we at last got permission to sail with 9 sail of the
line of Spanish Ships, it being just night when the last of the
Men of War got out of the harbour and the Remainder of
Fleet a Great way to Leeward and heavy sailers & not knowing where they were bound, I thought it best to Quit them and
make the best of my way. I therefore Spoke Capt Greene and
told him what I intended, at the same time ordered him to
make the best of his way and follow me. The next morning we

saw part of the fleet a Stern and at 10 O'clock lost Sight of
them, at 3 P.M saw the "Mintanzeys" under our Lee bow, at
same time saw Two Large Sail to Windward. Capt Greene
and Myself ageed they were British Cruizers. I then wore ship
and Stood for the Spanish fleet, as knowing it to be the only
way to save the "Duke de Luzerne." The Enemy making a
small angle on us if we kept our course, and Especially as er
might be obliged to haul up a Little to Clear Cape Florida and
the "Duke de Luzerne" sailing much heavier than us, at
10 O'Clock at night we made the Light of part of the Spanish
fleet. The Enemy then within Gun Shott, but as soon as they
saw the lights they left off chase, we kept in company with the
fleet all night. In the morning we found they were only 8 or
10 Sloops and Schooners, however they answered our Ends—
after speaking them and could find no account of the Men of
War we made the best of our Way, but finding the "Luzerne"
sailing much heavier than the "Alliance," it was agreed between Capt Greene, Mr. Brown and myself to have all the
publec money on board the "Alliance", as you will find by
Capt Greene's Letters. In the morning of the 20th we saw 3
Large Sail of Ships standing directly before us, the course
they were steering and the place they were in was a convincing
proof to me they were Enemys Ships especially as they wore
the same kind Vanes the Ships that chased us before had. I
then made a Signal for Capt Greene to make all the sail he
could & follow me, a short time after Capt Greene made a
Signal of superior force. I then made all the sail I could as not
having an idea of being any service to him, however some time
after about an hour, Capt Greene made a Signal to speak with
me, as I found I sailed faster than the Enemy, I shorten'd sail
and spoke to Capt Greene, one of the Enemys 32 Gun Frigates
then in Gun Shott of us, the other two but little way a Stern &
coming up fast with Capt Greene. I asked him what he wanted
he said they were Privateers, I told him he was mistaken &
I knew better—at my Dropping astern the Enemys head most
Frigate shorten'd sail & would not come near us, finding the two
Ships after coming up fast and confident within myself I must
fell a sacrifice if I stayed with Capt Greene. I told him I could
not stay by him, and the only chance he had to Get Clear was
to heave his guns overboard to lighten his ship & try them before the wind, the former he did, but kept his course, at that
time the second headmost Ship of the Enemy was within Gun
shott of the "Duc de Lauzun." I must not omit observing that

in the morning we saw a Ship to the Southwd of us who made sail and stood from us, altho Capt Greene & the headmost Ship fired several Shott at one another, but at too Great Distance to do Execution, it being the fault of the Enemy after telling Capt Green that I must leave him and in short at that time was determined as being of no service to him. Shortly after I saw the Strange Sail tack and stand for us as having all Reason in the world to suppose she was Stranger to the Enemy. Likewise at that time Capt Greene firing stern chasers at one of the Enemys Ships, & she firing bow chaces at him, the headmost and windmast of the Enemy then bore away across Capt Greene's Stern. I then ordered the Courses haul'd up and hard a weather the helm & Run Down between Capt Greene and the ship next to him in order to Give him a chance to get off by bringing the Enemy to Action which I did in a few moments Close on board for 45 Minutes, when The Enemy sheerd off, Capt Greene and myself hauld our wind for the strange sail who proved to be French 60 Gun Ship that sailed from the Havana two Days before us, and had on board half Million of Dollars and bound to some of the French Islands. During the Action my Officers and Men behaved well and altho but short I had ten wounded, one of which is since dead. My sails spars and Riging hurt a Little, but not so much but they would all do again. On the 18th at 10 P M. struck soundings off *Cape Hatterass*. I then spoke to Capt Greene and acquainted him with my having soundings, and at the same time ordered him to make all the sail he could and follow me. At 1 AM saw Capt Greene and in a Very little time lost sight of him, the Reason must be best known to him, as I am confident he might have kept company with us if he had a mind to and I not being off the Deck the whole night and did not carry more sail than he might have kept up with us. On the 19th at 6 PM off the *Capes of Delaware* after a thick Fogg, I fell in with two British Cruizers close on board them, one of them appeared to be a two Decker, the other a Twenty Gun Ship American Built, it blowing very had and Got thick of fogg soon after, and we Got clear, about 2 hours after we saw them again in a clear— having great Reason to suppose the coast was lined with the Enemys Ships, and no prospect of getting in till the Weather cleared up, I thought it best to bear away for this port where we anchor'd at three oclock this afternoon with 72 Thousand Dollars belonging to the public which I shall take care of till I have your orders what to do with it—however I do not think it very safe on board, and I have wrote to Mr. Geo. Olney at Provedence for him to come down here that I may consult with him Respecting the Safety of it.

The "Alliance" being arriv'd in America, and a number of her petty officers and mens time being out, they expect to be paid. In short if the Ship is not paid off as soon as possible. The Officers who are to stay by the Ship have been a Long time without Wages, they likewise expect to be paid off. In short if the Ship is not paid off and every man satisfyed she will lye a long time without men, to the contrary if they are Immediately paid I think we can be manned before the Ship is Repaired and I hope you will be pleased to give orders on that head.

The purser leaving his Ship in France and his Books being on Shore, I could not get his accounts before I sailed, nor had I got the Ships accounts from Mr. Barclay, but he promised to get the pursers accounts and send them with his own Respecting the Ship. In order to settle with the people it is required for me to have them both if they are come to hand as I suppose they are by Capt Barney you will please to send them by the first opportunity. I shall keep the Ship in Readiness as she came from the Sea till I have the pleasre to hear from you.

I must not omit to lett you know thst I want three Lieuts and a Master as soon as possible for I am almost worn out for want of assistance especially as I am obliged to let Capt Robt Caulfield whom I appointed first Lieut on the "Havana," and who has been of Great assistance to me on all occasions, should he incline to continue in the Navy, by Giving him a Commission you would make a good Officer and one that would be a credit to the service. If Capt Deal and Murryc, two Lieuts in the service & Mr Tanner late master of the "Confederacy" be in Phila and can be got, you would oblige me to appoint them to the Ship & send one or all of them here as soon as possible. If Capt Caulfield does not incline to come back, Capt Douglass of Trenton who came passenger with me and who I have a Great Opinion of will be pleased to appoint him a Liet. The Ship "Alliance" will want a Great Deal of Repairs, the sooner she gets them the better; you will pleased to give orders to somebody on that head. I was obliged to let Capt Greene have two of my Nine pounders, I want two in their place.

I have the honor to be with proper respect, Sir,

JOHN BARRY

Mate John Kessler's account of the Battle:

Hon Robt Morris

"March 7th, 1783. Sailed after taking on board a large quanity of Dollars and in company with the Continental ship "Luzerne" of 20 guns, Captain Green, who also had a quantity Dollars on board for Congress. We left Havana for the United States, after having taken on board between one and two hundred thousand dollars (specie) for Congress. On the passage one morning when it became light we discovered three Frigates right ahead within two leagues of us. The "Alliance" and "Luzerne" hove about and the three frigats gave us chase. The Alliance left them and the "Luzerne" fast, and Captain Barry seeing that they were gaining on the "Luzerne," we lay by for her to come up. The enemy also immediately lay by. When the "Luzerne" came up Captain Barry told Captain Greene to heave his guns overboard and put before the wind, while the "Alliance" would be kept by the wind that the "Luzerne" might escape. It was not probable that the enemy would attend most to the "Alliance," and the "Alliance" was out of danger in consequence of her superior sailing. Capt Green threw overboard all his guns but two or three, but instead of bearing away he got on our weather bow. A sail being observed on our weather bow standing towards us, Captain Barry hoisted a signal which was answered, and thereby Captain Barry knew her to be a French 50 gun ship from Havana, and he concluded to permit the enemy to come up under the assurance that the French ship would arrive and assist.

"Two of the enemy's ships kept at a distance on our weather quarter as if waiting to ascertain about the French ship, while the other was in our wake with topsails only and courses hauled, as was also the case with the "Alliance." The French ship approaching fast, Captain Barry went from gun to gun on the main deck, cautioning against too much haste and not to fire until the enemy was right abreast. He ordered the main topsail hove to the mast that the enemy (who had already fired a Bow gun, the shot of which struck into the cabin of the "Alliance") might come up as soon as he was abreast, when the action began, and before an half hour her guns were silenced and nothing but Musketry was fired from her. She appeared very much injured in her hull. She was of 32 guns and appeared very full of men, and after an action for 45 minutes She sheered off. Our injured was, I think 3 killed and 11 wounded (three of whom died of their wounds) and one sails and rigging cut. During all the action the French lay to as well as the enemy's ships."

As soon as the ship which we had engaged hove from us, her consorts joined her and all made sail, after which the French ship came down to us, and Captain Barry asked them why they did not come down during the action. They answered that they thought we might have been taken and the signal that known and the action only a sham to decoy him. His foolish idea thus perhaps lost us the three frigates, for Captain Barry's commencing the action was with the full expectation of the French ship joining and thereby not only be able to cope, but in fact subdue part, if not the whole, of them. The French Captain proposed, however, giving chase, which was done; but it soon appeared that his ship would not keep up with us, and the chase was given over.

"On the next morning it was proposed that, as the "Luzerne" was now unarmed, the public should be taken on board the "Alliance," which was accordingly done, together with Mr. John Brown, Secretary of the Board of Admiralty."

"On the remainder of the passage nothingworth noting Occurred, except that we became separated from the "LUZERNE." On the 20th of March we arrived at Newport, and on the 25th arrived at Providence in Rhode Island, when the crew were paid off and discharged."

The "Duc de Lauzun" succeeded in getting into Philadelphia off the Capes of the Delaware two British vessels barred the "ALLIANCE'S" way to entrance.

Mate Kessler erred in recording that John Brown was Transferred from the "Duc de Luzerne" to the Alliance with the cash.

On April 5th, Brown wrote Barry from Philadelphia, "I had the good luck to get in here the very day you got to Newport."

Barry replied from Providence River, April 19th, 1783:

"Happy for you, you had parted company with me. By that means you got in safe I was standing in for the Capes and had got seven fathoms of water on the five fathom bank when it cleared up and close on board of us was a two decker and a frigate. They immediately gave us chase and we run them into twenty fathoms water. In a short time it grew thick and we lost sight of them. I Then wore and stood in shore again.

"When we got in twelve fathoms they were the second time close on board of us and a little to the windward. I then bore away and they gave chase which left an opening for you to get in. It blew very hard and night coming on we soon lost sight of them. I have log myself and was going fourteen knots with a great deal of care."

The arrival of the "De Lauzun" is thus recorded in the Philadelphia Independent Gazette of March 22, 1783:

"Yesterday arrived here the ship "Duke de Luzan," Capt. Green, who left Havana on the 7th inst. in company with the "Alliance," Capt. Barry, and the Spanish squadron of ten sail of the line, gun boats, &c., destined for Porto Cabaldo in the Caraccas, where M. Vauderuil had arrived with his squadron and was in Hourly expectation on the arrival of the combined fleet from Europe. Advice of their sailing for the place of rendezvous is without doubt the object of these grand armament."

"A few days after the "Alliance" and the "Duke de Luzan parted from the fleet they fell in with three British frigates, two of which they engaged and beat off; the other did not come to action, the "Trition," a French, 64, and did not come winward, the enemy prudently retired." The same paper reported just one week later: "Last Thursday a gentleman arrived from Rhode Island with advice that the "Alliance" frigate, Capt. Barry, was arrived at Newport. She has had two severe actions on her passage from Havana with frigates of equal force. It is said she has brought a large sum of money on Government account."

"The "Alliance" frigate, Capt Barry is arrived at Newport in Rhode Island which she left in company with the ship "Duke de Lauzun" lately arrived here. On the 10th inst (three days after they left Havana) They fell in with three British frigates with whom they had an action in which the "Alliance" lost 11 men killed &c but we have no particulars of this affair.

Capt. Barry was chased on our coast by two frigates. Penna Packet March 29th 1783.

"The name of the English frigate with which the "Alliance" had had the "severe action" and the final Naval encounter of the War does not appear in any of the above of other contemporary reports. Nor does Mate Kessler mention it while Cooper's History of the Navy says "Even the name of the English ship appears to be lost" though in the later edition Cooper says James' History of the English Navy, "a very inaccurate authority" names "the "SIBYL" RATING 20 gun but mounting 28 commanded by Captain Vashon."

That is correct. It was the "Sybille," commanded by Captain Vashon. The "Sybille," a French ship of 38 guns and 350 men had, on January 22 of this year, been captured, in Lat. 36° 30′ by the "Hussay," 20 guns and 160 men, commanded by Thomas Macnamara Russell, and sent into New York, Arriving there on February 8. Captain Russell treated the captain of the "Sybille" some what harshly, claiming that he had shown false colors and a flag of distress in order to decoy the "Hussar," and had then fired upon her. Newspaper controversy concerning this allegation may be found in the Pennsylvania Journal of March 1, 1783, and reply thereto in the Royal Gazette of New York, March 8. The "Sybille" was added to the British Navy and departed to the southward, where she came in contact with the "Alliance" and Barry on March 10th 1783.

In Gouldsborough's Military and Naval Magazine it is related: "In 1802 an officer attached to Commodore Dale's squadron met with Captain Vashon, of the British Navy, at Gibraltar, and was informed by him that he commanded the English sloop of war "Sybil." Captain Vashon made the most respectful inquiries after Commodore Barry, and stated the facts, as they had been frequently related before by the Commodore himself; and in the most magnanimous terms accorded that

gallant officer a full and generous portion of his approbation, for the masterly manoeuvring of the "Alliance"
on that occasion.

"Captain Vashon stood high in the British navy as a
distinguished seaman, and observed that the commander
of the 74, who was then an admiral, spoke often to him on
the subject of their pursuit of the frigate "Alliance,"
always giving her commander great credit for his
conduct."

"Commodore Barry, on this as on all other occasions,
evinced his love of justice and spoke of Captain Vashon's
conduct, bravery and ability in terms of the highest
commendation."

In the Portfolio for July 1, 1813, it is stated that
Captain Vashon "confessed he had never seen a ship so
ably fought as the "Alliance;" that he has never before
"received such a drubbing and that he was indebted to
the assistance of his consorts."

"The coolness and intrepidity, no less than the skill
and fertility in expedients, which Captain Barry displayed on this occasion, are described in naval annals as
truly wonderful: every quality of a great naval commander was brought out with extraordinary brilliancy."

"It was when hailed on this occasion that Barry
answered: "The United States ship "Alliance," saucy
Jack Barry—half Irish and half Yankee—who are you?"
No authority for the statement is given. Barry is not
likely to have indulged in such bombast."

The story of "The Last Battle of the Revolution"
which all Publications have assigned to March, 1783, is
thus related in Abbot's "Blue Jackets of '76."

"Once more, before the cessation of hostilities between Great Britain and the United States threw her out
of commission, did the "Alliance" exchange shots with a
hostile man-of-war. It was in 1782 (ought to be March,
1783) when the noble frigate was engaged in bringing

specie from the West Indies. She had under convoy a
vessel loaded with supplies, and the two had hardly left
Havana when some of the enemy's ships caught sight of
them and gave chase. While the chase was in progress a
50 gun ship hove in sight, and was soon made out to be a
French frigate, Feeling that he had an ally at hand, Barry
now wore ship, and attacked the leading vessel, and a
spirited action followed, until the enemy, finding himself hard pressed, signalled, for his consorts and Barry,
seeing that the French ship made no sign of coming to his
aid, drew off."

"Irritated by the failure of the French frigate to come
to his assistance Barry bore down upon her and hailed.
The French captain declared that the manoeuvres of the
"Alliance" and his antagonist had made him suspect that
the engagement was only a trick to draw him into the
power of the British fleet. He had feared that the "Alliance" had been captured, and was being used as a
decoy; but now that matter was made clear to him, he
would join the "Alliance" in pursuit of the enemy. This
he did; but Barry soon found that the fifty was so slow a
sailer that the "Alliance" might catch up with the
British fleet, and be knocked to pieces by their guns
Before the Frenchman could get within range.

Accordingly Barry abandoned the chase and renewed
his homeward course. This engagement was the last
fought by the "Alliance" during the Revolution and with
it we practically complete our narrative of the work of
the regular navy during that war."

The above quotations from Barry's own Report and
letters, Mate Kessler's Records, Abbot's "Blue Jackets,"
Gouldsborough's Military and naval Magazine as well
as extracts from the "Portfolio" for July 1st 1813, these
abstracts have been used to bring the reader in close contact with the direct witnesses of the Last Battle of the
Revolution which not only gave due honor to Barry's

seamanship but also saved the funds from Havana which were used as the foundation capital for the Bank of North America in Philadelphia. The author of this volume respectfully credits the historian Martin Griffin's "Commodore John Barry"—1903 with this valuable and informative material for this Last Sea Battle of the Revolution.

CHAPTER X

Barry Aids Constitution's Ratification
December 12th 1787

The days of Barry's glory were days of sorrow for Jones who during the years 1783 to 1785 had been seriously ill. Jones lived in Philadelphia and Bethlehem where he gradually regained strength and then appealed to Congress for an appointment to settle the question of all war prizes taken in Europe under his own command. Congress acquiesced to his desires and Jones remained in Europe until 1787 to complete the task assigned to him. During this period of time we find Barry busily engaged in commercial transportation for the government, especially in clearing America's debt to Holland through the transportation of tobacco from Virginia to Holland. When Barry's ship the "Alliance" was sold in 1785 and the country was left without a navy, Barry entered politics in Philadelphia and strove to stabilize the country's legislation which would guarantee permanent peace.

The Federal Convention held in Philadelphia in 1787 formulated a Constitution whereby the State could form "a more perfect union" and "promote domestic tranquility" and the Assembly was notified to convene. The next morning the "honorable delegates led by Benjamin Franklin were ushered into the Hall of Assembly, their report was made and they presented the new Constitution." Action was delayed and when the ratification was referred to a convention of citizens, it was resolved to call a State Convention. When again assembled, nineteen members who voted against the adoption of the new Constitution, were absent. Chaos reigned supreme

JOHN BARRY
1745–1801

and Barry was highly incensed and aroused to action. Barry and others sympathetic to the adoption of the Constitution organized themselves into a group called "the Compellers" and went out and physically brought enough members into the meeting to form a necessary quorum. They dragged the seceders to the State House and thrust them into the chamber where the Assembly was in session without a quorum. The vote was finally obtained and the date of the Convention fixed. The people crowded inside and outside the building cheered, Christ Church bells rang, and Captain Barry was victor over indifference and postponement of action. Within 23 hours after the Constitutional Convention had adjourned, the Assembly of Pennsylvania called a Convention to act upon it. Thanks to the ardent zeal of Barry—a Captain without a ship who wished to make America a land of imperishable liberty! On December 12th 1787 the Federal Constitution was ratified!

Jones Decamps to Russia

In the midst of political chaos and the final ratification of the Constitution Barry remained close to Washington and his ideals. Jones returned to Philadelphia after his settlement of the problems of war prizes in Europe and was awarded a gold medal by Congress for his victory at sea at Flamborough off the coast of England on September 23rd 1779—when the "Bonnhomme Richard" defeated the "Serapis." Jones had been honored abroad and at home as a superb fighter and sea-captain, but he was frustrated because Congress had not elevated him to the honor of an American Rear-Admiral which he so vehemently desired. Insatiable for more horizons and more fields of war to conquer, Jones offered his service to Queen Catherine II of Russia in her war against the Turks.

Peace and Commerce

The direct effect of the cessation of hostilities of the Revolutionary War was the opening of the Atlantic Ocean for immediate maritime trade. Washington's ideal of the open seas gave courage to the entire world and little did men, who had fought and bled for American Independence and Freedom, dream of the impending storms and battles of the War of 1812 which would retrieve on land and sea the peace of 1783.

As early as May 2nd 1783, the "Hibernia" from Dublin arrived in the port of Philadelphia. The cargo of this ship which enjoyed the first free passage of the seas was described as consisting of gold and silver, silks, rich brocades, flowered Mantuas and Fabrics, colored tissues and Florentines, tamboured silk and satin for gentlemen's vests and black Norwich Capes, all of which were later found on sale in the well known store of Clement Biddle of Philadelphia.

The two valiant seamen—Barry and Jones—were separated forever! Jones became Rear-Admiral of the Russian Fleet in the Black Sea under Queen Catherine II of Russia! Barry remained faithful until death—a friend of Washington and an immortal American!

Reconnaissance

BARRY	JONES
1783–Jan. 8th–Barry sailed from Martinco.	1783–Jan.–Jones in Bay of Fundy, San Juan, Puerto Rico, Cape Francois. "Burgoyne" with 74 guns run on rocks and was totally destroyed and lost with over 200 officers and men lost.
Jan. 22nd–Off Hispanola.	
Feb. 3rd–Peace Treat Ratified.	
March 10th–Last Battle of Revolution. The "Alliance" with Barry in command contacted British ship "Sybille"	Feb.–"Triomphante" arrived in Porto Cabello where she was joined by other members of the fleet.

Reconnaissance

BARRY

which Captain Vashon commanded. Vashon confessed that never before he "received such a drubbing" and never saw a ship so ably fought as the "Alliance." "The coolness and intrepidity, no less than the skill and fertility in expedients, which Barry displayed on the occasion, are described in naval annals as truly wonderful; every quality of a great naval commander was brought out with extraordinary brilliancy." Thus the "Alliance" fought the last battle of the Revolution and also saved the money removed from the "Lazun" which funds were used to found the Bank of North America in Philadelphia.

April 4th–Aboard the "Alliance", Barry writes letters from Pautuxet, Mass. and Providence, Rhode Island.

June 10th–Barry went to New York where he saw the "Sybille" which bore the marks of injury inflicted upon it by the "Alliance" Barry was ordered to go to Virginia with the "Alliance" and transport tobacco to Holland. When loaded, the "Alliance" leaked and Barry unloaded the tobacco and made the necessary repairs at a cost of $6,000.00. The tobacco was used as part-payment of America's debt to Holland.

JONES

Feb. 18th–Jones fell sick and dangerously ill.

March 16th–Jones purchased confiscated estate near Newark, N. J. as place of retirement in old days.

May 18th–Jones sick in Philadelphia.

June 5th–Jones a patient of Moravian Hospital in Bethlehem for hydrotherapy and treatment of his ailments.

Nov. 1st–Jones appealed to Congress for an appointment as agent for all prizes taken in Europe under his own command. Congress passed an Act favorable for such a commission.

Nov. 10th–Jones sailed from Philadelphia in packet "Washington" for France.

Nov. 30th–Jones landed in Plymouth, England.

Dec. 20th–Jones introduced to King of France and began negotiations for settlement of the Prizes of War.

Reconnaissance

BARRY	JONES
1784–Feb. 1st–Barry in Philadelphia Wages paid by government to Captain Barry $60.00. per month.	1784–May 18th–Jones appeals for final settlement.
	Oct. 23rd–In Statements a re-partitioning of Prizes issued.
Oct. 18th–Barry in Baltimore. Brought the "Alliance" from Havana.	
Nov. 16th–Barry writes "I know not whether I am connected with Maryland or Pennsylvania, but it makes little odds by which I am paid, so I get my due."	
Sept. 28th–Barry sent message Congress Asking for "equal justice" for the sailors and soldiers of the war. The peace of 1783 found the finances of the Government altogether unequal to the support of the navy. Most of the public cruisers had fallen into the hands of the enemy or had been destroyed and the few that remained were sold. The "Alliance" was a favorite ship to the last, but was reluctantly disposed of to avoid the expense of repairs.	
1785–Jan. 12th–Barry lived in Strawberry Hill Home in Philadelphia.	1785–July 29th–Final settlement of War prizes effected by Jones.
	August 20th–Jones arrived in London from Paris.
June 19th–"Alliance" sold for $7,700.00. Barry had first and last command of Continental vessels. No Navy.	
Dec. 19th–Barry in Philadelphia, Boston, New York and brief visit to Ireland.	

Reconnaissance

BARRY	JONES
1786–Nov. 2nd–Letters sent to Barry from New York office of accounts, Marine Department.	
1787–May–Sixth Article of Constitution adopted.	1787–Oct. 11th–Congress approved Jones settlement of War Prizes and awarded a gold medal for valour and brilliant service in battle off the coast of Great Britain to Chevalier John Paul Jones.

BARRY

1786–Nov. 2nd–Letters sent to Barry from New York office of accounts, Marine Department.

1787–May–Sixth Article of Constitution adopted.

June 11th–Barry actively promotes the ratification of the Constitution formulated by Federal Convention. Barry zealous of procuring "the more perfect union" of the States whose independence he had been so helpful in achieving.

Sept. 17–Work of ratification was completed because Barry led a group of "compellers" to visit the homes of the seceders who shirked their responsibility. These men were dragged to the State House and thrust into the chamber where the Assembly was in session. The vote was obtained and the date of the Convention was fixed. The people cheered, bells rang and Barry was happy for within 23 hours after the Constitutional Convention had adjourned, the Assembly of Pennsylvania had called a Convention to act on it. Barry deserved credit for forcing this necessary issue of the times.

Dec. 12th–Federal Constitution ratified.

Dec. 22nd–Frigate "Alliance" under the name of the "Indiaman" sailed for Canton with Captain Read in Command.

JONES

1787–Oct. 11th–Congress approved Jones settlement of War Prizes and awarded a gold medal for valour and brilliant service in battle off the coast of Great Britain to Chevalier John Paul Jones.

Nov. 11th–Jones left New York for service in the Russian Navy in the Black Sea. Went to Dover, Eng., then to Copenhagen, Paris and finally to St. Petersburg, Russia.

CHAPTER XI

Jones Becomes Russian Rear-Admiral
May 26th 1788

Why did Jones leave America for the Russian Navy and care-free Paris? The years 1788 to 1793 were marked by a severe differential of human interest in American Independence by Barry and Jones. Barry's vigorous life was devoted one hundred percent to his American citizenship and he led an active civic life in Philadelphia until September 13th 1803. Jones, on the other hand, left America and on May 26th 1788 received the honors which he sought under the despotic and murderous Queen Catherine II of Russia as a Rear-Admiral—Kontra-admiral Pavel Ivanovich Jones. Jones found the two years of his service in the Black Sea turbulent because of the many free-lance officers who competed with him for honors in driving off the Turkish Squadron in the Liman Campaign. The last three years of Jones' life spent in Paris were most disheartening and on July 18th 1792 at the early age of forty-five years, he died in his rented compartment at 19 Rue Tournon in Paris. We shall not explain the amorous bachelor life of Jones who truthfully never married because he was jilted by Miss Dorothea Dandridge who married the illustrious Virginian orator, Patrick Henry, the Governor of Virginia, and neither shall we minimize nor depreciate the heroic qualities and leadership found in his personality as a superb seaman.

While Jones was engaged in the settlement of war-prizes in Europe, service in Russia and leisure in Paris, Barry spent his time from 1785 to 1792 in the pursuit of

Grave of Commodore John Barry, St. Mary's Church Cemetery, 250 South 4th Street, Philadelphia, Pa.

better treatment by the government for soldiers and sailors, both in the service and in the days of their honorable discharge from the service. He was constantly alert to the needs of a permanent American Navy and worked incessantly for it. In spite of his many disappointments, Barry was famous for saying that "America is the best place under the sun." He openly professed his Catholic faith, mingled with everybody and understood the weakness of human nature. It is noteworthy that Admiral Samuel Eliot Morison, U.S.N., in his historical masterpiece "John Paul Jones—A Sailor's Biography" honestly credits Barry as being "the most popular Captain in the Navy." Whilst in Philadelphia, Barry lived in the heart of the busy city and also in the historic dwelling known as "Strawberry Mansion." He participated in the relief work involved in the Yellow Fever epidemic of 1793 and survived the dreadful disaster in which over four thousand persons died.

The Catholics of America knew America and loved it. They also knew of the part which their church had played in assisting the cause of American Independence and gave Washington as their General, Commander in Chief of both the Army and Navy and President of the United States of America, the proper respect and honor which he rightly deserved. Noteworthy was the following Message of December 1789 from the American Catholics to Washington:

"It is your peculiar talent, in war and in peace, to afford security to those who commit their protection into your hands. In war you shield them from the ravages of armed hostility; in peace, you establish public tranquility, by the justice and moderation, not less than by the vigor, of your government. By example, as well as by vigilance, you extend the influence of laws on the manners of our fellow-citizens.

"You encourage respect for religion; and inculcate, by words and actions, that principle, on which the welfare of nations so much depends, that a superintending Providence governs the events of the world, and watches over the conduct of men. Your exalted maxims, and unwearied attention to the moral and physical improvement of our country, have produced already the happiest effects. . . .

"This prospect of national prosperity is peculiarly pleasing to us, on another account; because, whilst our country preserves her freedom and independence, we shall have a well founded title to claim from her justice, equal rights of citizenship, as the price of our blood spilt under your eyes, and of our common exertions for her defence, under your auspicious conduct—rights rendered more dear to us by the remembrance of former hardships. . . .

"When we solicit the protection of Heaven over our common country, we neither omit, nor can omit recommending your preservation to the singular care of Divine Providence; because we conceive that no human means are so available to promote the welfare of the United States, as the prolongation of your health and life, in which are included the energy of your example, the wisdom of your counsels, and the persuasive eloquence of your virtues."

Noteworthy also was the reply of President Washington to the loyal Catholic Americans of the same uncertain and troubled years of the nation:

"I feel that my conduct, in war and in peace, has met with more general approbation, than could reasonably have been expected; and I find myself disposed to consider that fortunate circumstance, in a great degree resulting from the able support, and extraordinary candour, of my fellow-citizens of all denomination. . . .

"America, under the smiles of Divine Providence—the protection of a good Government—the cultivation of manners, morals, and piety—can hardly fail of attaining an uncommon degree of eminence in literature, commerce, agriculture, improvements at home, and respectability abroad.

"As mankind becomes more liberal, they will be more apt to allow, that all those who conduct themselves, as worthy members of the community, are equally entitled to the protection of civil Government. I hope ever to see America among the foremost nations in examples of justice and liberality. And I *presume that your fellow-citizens will not forget the patriotic part, which you took in the accomplishment of their Revolution, and the establishment of their Government—or the important assistance which they received from a nation in which the Roman Catholic religion is professed.* . . .

"While my life and my health shall continue, in whatever situation I may be, it shall be my constant endeavour to justify the favourable sentiments which you are pleased to express of my conduct. And may the members of your Society in America animated alone by the pure spirit of Christianity, and still conducting themselves as the faithful subjects of our free Government, enjoy every temporal and spiritual felicity."

Reconnaissance

BARRY	JONES
1788–Jan. 7th–Barry goes to China on Merchant Ship "Asia."	1788–Jan.–Jones in Copenhagen.
	Feb.–Jones left Paris.
1789–April 30th–Washington elected President. Barry offers services to President Washington in case of war with Algerines.	May 26th–Assumed command of Russian Fleet. Assumed command and hoisted his flag as Rear-Admiral of the ship "Wolodimer" under Queen Catherine II of Russia. Met with a cabal of Brigadier Alexiano and other commanders against his authority. Advanced against the Turkish Fleet of 57 vessels.
	June 16th–Turkish Fleet attacks Jones under walls of of Oczakow but Turks lost battle. Victory of Liman.
	June 27th–Sailed to Kinburn and Danube River.
	July 31st–Turkish Fleet again appears at Beresane.
	Nov. 4th–Turkish Fleet retired to Constantinople.

Reconnaissance

BARRY	JONES
	Dec. 28th–Jones appeared in court before Queen Catherine who promised Jones a better position than that of the Black Sea. Conspiracy to ruin Jones thwarted. Jones left Warsaw for Amsterdam. Wrote to Washington and stated that if property could be purchased for him in Lancaster, he would return to America.
1789–June 4th–Barry returns from China to Philadelphia.	1789–Jones in St. Petersburg and Warsaw. Dec. 20th–In Amsterdam.
1790–June 24th–Barry asks for some emoluments to Navy Men as were already granted to army men.	1790–June 1st–Jones left Amsterdam and went to England and finally to Paris. July 9th–From Paris, Jones wrote to Baron de Grim that he desired to cling to Russian engagements. Jones lives in Paris.
1791–Barry participates in civic life and political progress in Philadelphia.	1791–From Paris Jones writes of poor health to his sisters and Colonel Blackden.
1792–Barry resides in Strawberry Mansion in Fairmount Park, Philadelphia. Dec. 6th–In a letter of this date, Barry writes "America is the best country."	1792–June 1st–President Washington commissioned Jones to negotiate with the Dey of Algeria concerning ransom of American citizens in captivity and "to conclude and sign a Convention there upon."
1793–Oct. 20th—Yellow fever rages in Philadelphia and over four thousand died.	June 2nd–Jones appointed "American Consul for Algeria" by Washington. July 6th–Jones 45 years of age. July 18th–Jones was seized with jaundice to which dropsy fol-

Reconnaissance

BARRY	JONES
	lowed and died at Rue de Tournon, Paris, 3rd floor apartment.
	July 18th–Ambassador Morris obtained permission from Commissary Sommoneau that Jones body be buried without charge in a pauper's grave. Simmoneau answered by paying for the funeral and embalming it, "so that, if America ever changed her mind, it will be possible to correct this awful blunder."
	July 20–The body of Jones was placed in a leaden coffin in case the United States should claim his remains. The place of internment was not recorded and therefore caused much trouble to locate the body 113 years after his death. An attempt was made to locate the grave for 7 years by General Horace Porter, Ambassador to France. Jones body was finally found and brought to America with proper honors and burial at Annapolis, Md.

CHAPTER XII

U.S. Navy Commission No. 1 Goes to Barry June 14th 1794

The war prizes taken and the battles won on the seas of warfare did not win for Barry the title of "Father of the American Navy." These achievements are expected of our Naval heroes! The reason for Barry's distinctive title of honor can be found in his accreditation of naval rating and service. On official record are these facts:

1st: From 1760 to 1775: Both Barry and Jones were employees of American Commercial fleets.

2nd: October 13th 1775: Congress resolved to purchase 2 ships and fit them for the defense of America. The Marine Committee under this Resolve of Continental Congress bought two vessels and named them the "Lexington" and the "Reprisal."

The ship over which Barry was formerly Captain, namely, the "Black Prince" was also purchased and re-named the "Alfred."

3rd: December 7th 1775: The "Lexington" which was a separate and independent command was placed in the hands of Barry with the commission of Captain.

The "Reprisal" was also a separate and independent command under the orders of the Marine Committee, was placed in the hands of Captain Wickes.

The "Alfred" was under the command of Commander Hopkins as part of his fleet and commissioned to the "Alfred" were Captain Salonstall and 1st Lieutenant Jones.

4th: October 10th 1776: With the First Re-organization of the American Navy, the official listing

Sarcophagus of John Paul Jones, Crypt of Naval Academy Chapel, Annapolis, Md.

was Barry as No. 7 and Jones as No. 18. Barry therefore had a higher listing and superior ship. At this time both men were Captains. Barry commanded the "Effingham" of 28 guns and Jones commanded the Sloop "Providence" of 12 guns and later the "Alfred" of 30 guns. Jones openly and vehemently protested his humiliation against Barry's superior rating.

5th: June 14th 1794: Barry was given "Commission No. 1" which was personally conferred upon Barry by President Washington on Feb. 22nd 1797 "by and with the advice and consent of the Senate."

These high ratings came to Barry without solicitation and were merited. As far as lengths of years in the American Navy is concerned, Barry served for 43 years and Jones rendered 13 years of naval service. Barry appeared before Congress and the Maritime Committee on behalf of justice and equity towards the rank and file of the army and navy, but never did he appeal and protest as Jones did solely for his promotion as a Rear-Admiral and Head of the American Navy. As early as 1781 did Jones manifest his personal ambition for glory and honor when he declared that "rank opens the door to glory."

Due credit must be given to Jones for his magnificent battle off Flamborough when the wounded and dying "Bonhomme Richard" almost miraculously arose to the full power of its resurrection and from destruction and death, conquered the "Serapis" and British fleet on September 23rd 1779. This victory can be truly called the height of Jones' professional success! The exploits and accomplishments in the defense of America by Jones must also be given due credit, but the sum total of all these achievements do not make him the "Father of the American Navy." The greatest enemies of Jones were within the psychological realm of his proud personality. As a matter of record, Captain James Nicholson in a personal

letter to Barry on June 24th 1781 congratulates Barry
and told him about the personal applications of Jones
to the members of Congress to have himself made "Head
of the Navy" He told Barry that "your arrival and success
came opportunely and I did not fail to make use of it in
the presence of Captain Jones and his advocates by observing that you had acquitted yourself well, which they
acknowledged. I then told them they could not do less
than make you also an "Admiral" to which I had not a
sentence in reply. It irritated Jones so much that he was
obliged to decamp." (Barnes 855—Griffin 149).

It must also be remembered that whilst Barry was held
by many as the "Head of the Navy," in that very year of
1781 the Admiralty and Navy Boards were abolished by
Congress. Naval affairs were solely in the hands of the
Finance Department which was directed by Robert
Morris who notified Barry on September 21st 1781, that
the only two frigates remaining were the "Deane" and
the "Alliance." These two vessels were to be under Barry's
command for the purpose of disturbing the enemy and
"to do honor to the American Flag." This meagre honor
placed immense responsibilities upon Barry!

Apart from these superior naval ratings of Barry,
let us say a few words about the War Prizes of the
Revolutionary War. Who brought into Philadelphia the
first British ship as a war prize? Captain Barry was the
first Commander appointed under the direct authority
of the Continental Congress. He was also appointed to the
first Continental armed Cruiser "Lexington," named
after the battle place of the Revolution, which was fitted
out under Continental authority by the Marine Committee. As Captain of this cruiser, he brought into port of
Philadelphia the first War Prize, namely the British
Vessel "Edward," on April 7th 1776. The "Lexington"
at that time was flying the Continental or Union Flag of
America.

From these few vessels the American or United States Navy began! It is little wonder that the generic term "Father of the American Navy" was applied to Barry; however, it could be justly applied to General George Washington, who immediately after the Battle of Lexington on April 19th 1775 and at Cambridge on July 15th 1775, publicly and humbly assumed the responsibility of his work and leadership as "Commander-in-Chief of the Armies of the United Colonies on land and sea." We could easily dismiss the literary and symbolical paternity of the American Navy by assigning, as some writers have proposed, the title of "Father of the American Navy" to General George Washington, but a rhetorical compromise would not end the discussion which the enemies of Barry inaugurated many years ago.

In order to better understand how the evolution of the American Navy was accomplished, we may assume that General Washington was the dynamic power under which Barry studied, worked and served America in the formation, growth and development of the American Navy. Let us present this brief resume and then close this chapter with our usual reconnaissance:

Please remember that the American Revolution began with no armed vessels. Rhode Island, as early as August 1775, began a type of naval defense by fitting out small schooners to defend the Atlantic Coast trade. The Colony of Connecticut also had two vessels for the same protective service. In December 1775, Congress recommended several vessels and to Rhode Island must go the credit of having recommended to Congress the foundation of an American Navy for the United Colonies. In the spring of 1776 Massachusetts fitted out some vessels for sea defense. General Washington naturally regarded these various types of naval defense as part of the army until Congress made the proper laws which brought the American Navy into existence. You will remember that

on November 16th 1775 the first Marine Corps was appointed by Congress and the so-called Marine Committee under the authority of Continental Congress
purchased the first two vessels called the "Lexington"
and the "Reprisal" and the famous "Black Prince" of
Barry's was re-named the "Alfred." Barry was named
Captain of the "Lexington;" Wickes was Captain of the
"Reprisal" and Jones was 1st Lieutenant under Captain
Salonstall of the "Alfred." This fundamental rating was
simultaneously made official on Dec. 7th 1775. Ships
were constructed, purchased and navigated by the
youthful American Navy. Many American ships were
captured and also burned by the British. On June 3rd
1785 there no longer existed an American Navy. Even
the "Alliance" was sold on August 1st 1785.

Barry, however, never relinquished his ideals of
possessing an American Navy and also of building Navy
Yards as bases for the ships. Out of all this endeavor and
patriotic enthusiasm of Washington and Barry a new
Navy arose! On March 19th 1794 Barry wrote to Washington and offered himself to organize the Navy and
command a squadron against the Algerians. On April
12th 1794 official orders were given for the construction
of a new ship to be called the "United States" to which
important work Barry was assigned on August 4th 1794.
Barry immediately went to Georgia to select timber for
the new ship and the site for construction was named as
the Delaware River at the foot of Washington Street.

While in the preparation of this major operation of
ship building, Barry received a surprise on June 14th
1794 when he was named by President Washington the
ranking Naval officer with Commission No. 1, the formal
acceptance of which took place on Washington's Birth-
day, February 22nd 1797. Barry wrote to Washington as
of June 6th 1794. "The honor done me in appointing me
a Commander in the Navy of the United States is grate-

fully acknowledged and accepted by your most obedient and humble servant—John Barry." It was on July 1st 1794 that Barry signed the "Oath of Fidelity" and continued with his plans for the construction of the "United States" which construction continued for two years until May 10th 1797 when in the presence of over two thousand people at the foot of Washington Street on the shores of the Delaware, the noble and first Frigate of the new Navy yet incomplete was launched.

On July 3rd 1797, the Hon. Benjamin Stoddard, the new Secretary of the new Navy under President Adams, ordered Barry to proceed to sea and to cruise from Cape Henry to Nantucket "to subdue, seize and take any armed French vessel which should be found within the jurisdictional limits of the United States or elsewhere on the high seas, with apparel, guns and appurtenances." He was also ordered to take with him the "Delaware" under Captain Decatur, the "Herald" under Captain Sever and a revenue cutter of 14 guns from Boston "and to proceed to the West Indies" where the French ships were assembled for no good purposes.

Naval Protection Against French Raiders

Barry was honored with the command of the "United States" which he personally constructed and which cost the youthful nation the sum of $299,336.00. In the autumn of 1798, Barry cruised from the Delaware along the eastern coastline northward while Decatur cruised from the Delaware to Cape Henry, the most prominent captured vessels or "war prizes" were the French Schooner "La Jaleux" of 14 guns and 70 men with the sloop "Gadaloupe" with 14 guns and 67 men. On November 15th, Barry was ordered to New Hampshire and Decatur to the Chesapeake.

The establishment of the new American Navy brought joy to Barry and on Nov. 29th he was officially asked to submit to Congress his own ideas and a "system for the government of the Navy." As of Dec. 7th 1798 Barry was placed in immediate command of the "United States," "Constitution," "George Washington" and the "Merryman" for the West Indies in active operation for the protection of our commerce, for the destruction of French Cruising vessels which were armed and cruising from St. Christopher's as far as the Barbadoes and Tobago. The primary objective was to relieve commerce from the precarious pirates who continually cruised from the Island of Guadaloupe. Barry's fleet in part consisted of these vessels which Secretary Stoddard said "must claim your attention:"

"United States"	"John Adams"
"Constitution"	"Congress"
"George Washington"	"Little Adams"
"Mereman"	"Little York"
"Portsmouth"	"Connecticut"
"Pickering"	"Boston"
"Eagle"	"General Green"
"Herald"	"Siren"
"Scommel"	"Enterprise"
"Dickgrove"	"Argosy"

Another interesting raid by Barry was made on February 3rd 1799, when the "United States" chased a French privateer "Amour de la Patrie." A ball was sent through her hull so that she quickly began to fill and settle. Barry sent Decatur to rescue the crew of the sinking ship, after which the "Mereman" captured "LaBuefort de Phenix" of 14 guns and the "La Magiciese" of 14 guns. The "Portsmouth" captured the "La Bonapart" "Le Bullsate," "La Tripos" and the "Le Bon Pere." Barry's success humiliated France and on September 30th 1799,

France through the French Consul Bonaparte signed a Treaty of Peace with the United States of America which opened the sea to Commerce and Navigation between America and the world.

With the inauguration of Thomas Jefferson as the third President of the United States, Barry was ordered to bring the "United States" Frigate to Washington, D.C. on March 23rd. The Navy was then placed on a Peace Basis and Barry was engaged solely in proving guns cast by Mr. Lane in the vicinity of Philadelphia, and later at Colonel Hughes' works at Havre de Grace, Maryland. In August 1802, a Board of Examiners for applicants for commissions in the Navy was organized with Barry, Dale and Bainbridge as directors.

Devoted to his family and the spiritual interests of the Catholic Church, Barry acted as sponsor on October 19th 1802 for the baptism of Isaac Austin Hayes in St. Mary's Church of Philadelphia. On November 24th, the Secretary of the Navy sent to Barry an impression of a golden medal presented to Captain Truxton for his gallantry. The Secretary explicitly said "Considering you the Senior Officer of the Navy and entitled to the most respectful consideration, I cannot resist the inclination I feel at present of presenting one to you."

With a keen realization that even to men constantly in prominent positions and in the service of their country, death inevitably delivers the summons to them which brings them before their Creator and Judge in eternity, Barry made his Last Will and Testament on February 27th 1803 and on September 13th of the same year, after a prolonged illness, he died in his home on Strawberry Hill, Philadelphia. The funeral cortege moved from his city home at 186 Chestnut Street to Saint Mary's Catholic Church on South Fourth Street, where a Requiem Mass was celebrated for his spiritual repose and his body was buried with naval honors in the adjoining cemetery. His grave is located near to the graves of Captain John Rosseter, Captain Thomas Fitzsimmons and the Patriot George Meade. The Epitaph which was an eloquent eulogy written by the eminent non-Catholic Dr. Benjamin Rush, M.D. a signer of the Declaration of Independence, will be found in the following chapter of this monogram.

The historical hiatus from Barry's internment to Jones disinterment was exactly 105 years (1792 to 1897) or from the time of Jones death and burial in Paris until the finding and bringing of his body to Annapolis, 113 years elapsed. General Horace Porter, a West Point graduate and ambassador to France, organized a search in 1899 for the body of Jones. The body was found intact and well preserved and the record definitely states "we immediately exclaimed 'Paul Jones!' " and all the witnesses "around the coffin removed their hats, feeling that they were in the presence of the illustrious dead" gave solemn testimony that at last justice was to shown to an American hero. On April 20th 1905 the body of Jones was newly prepared for its entombment and placed temporarily in the vault of the American Church of the Holy Trinity in Paris.

On July 6th 1905 the body was borne in procession along the Champs Elysees, Paris, and then conveyed by Admiral Sigsbee and a squadron of warships to America. The escort consisted of the "Brooklyn," "Tacoma," "Chattanooga" and "Galveston" under orders from President Theodore Roosevelt, Commander-in-Chief of the United States Navy. With due honors, the body was brought in 1906 to the Naval Academy at Annapolis; services were held in Dahlgren Hall and finally his remains were interred in the sarcophagus of the Memorial Tomb in the basement of the Naval Academy Chapel in the year 1913. The sculptor, Sylvian Salieres, carved the sarcophagus, the dolphins on which it rests and the eight monolithic columns surrounding it; the material is "Grand Antique des Pyrenese" marble, in compliment to France. Ernest Flagg, the architect of the new Naval Academy, chose the design for the Chapel Dome partly resembling that of the Hotel des Invalides in Paris, which contains the remains of Napoleon. Visitors to the Annapolis Naval Academy honor Jones by visiting his magnificent last resting place and feel that justice has been shown to one who fought bravely for American Independence. The neglect of past years is compensated by the glory of the present tomb of Jones in Annapolis, Maryland, whilst the many monuments which radiate from the simple grave of Barry in St. Mary's Graveyard, Philadelphia, also give honor to one whom justice proclaims "the Father of the American Navy."

CHAPTER XIII

Well Done! The Accolade of Merit and Justice

As a term of high accreditation, the words "Well Done" were used in the Old Testament by the Divine Psalmist David. In the New Testament we find Our Divine Redeemer, Jesus Christ, applying these words to the faithful and worthy servant of His parable of doctrine and morality. In the United States Navy, seamen have been often rewarded by their superior officers with the well known citations of merit and medals of honor, but the words "Well Done" have always crowned the ceremonial for our American Heroes. In the same sense, we desire to apply honor and glory to the two distinguished seamen of this historical narrative. Both deserve the encomium of all known or unknown heroes who fought for American Independence. However, there is a time for reconnaissance and judgment in which we must see clearly the differentials of service and acknowledge seniority of rank, priority of subaltern and administrative service, as well as superiority of personality for the crowning act of reason and logic in determining who was rightly "the Father of the American Navy".

You, dear reader, shall be your own judge in this historical case of Barry and Jones. The author "with charity for all and malice towards none", has the privilege of making his own decision. After a thorough study of all the historical facts which have been assembled in this monograph, the writer had decided that the greater good for the procurement of American Independence was achieved by Commodore John Barry and to him should go the title of "Father of the American Navy".

Commodore Barry Monument, Fairmount Park, Philadelphia, Pa.

The differentials of personality and the accomplishments of "greater good" for American Independence can be summarized in the following symbolical accolade of historical truth:

1st: Birth and Death:
>Barry was born in Ireland in 1745 and died in Philadelphia in 1803.
>
>Jones was born in Scotland in 1747 and died in Paris in 1792.

2nd: Religion:
>Barry was baptized Roman Catholic and died as a practical Catholic.
>
>Jones was baptized Presbyterian but made Masonry his life's religion.

3rd: Patriotism:
>Barry manifested 15 years of loyalty to Ireland and 43 years of service for American Freedom and Independence.
>
>Jones showed loyalty to Scotland and England for 26 years, 15 years of service he rendered for American Freedom, 2 years he was allegiant to Queen Catherine in the Russian Navy and finally spent the last two years of his life in Paris.

4th: Education:
>In addition to his elementary schooling, Barry was skilled in navigation; his letters were brief; he was communicative and popular; he kept simple records of his grestest achievements; loved hard work and family life.
>
>Jones was a student of literature; prolific writer and fearless speaker; and loved the social and diplomatic life of his times.

5th: Physical health:
>Barry possessed good health and modestly conserved it.
>
>Jones in youth was vigorous but dissipated his last years.

6th: Psychoanalysis:
        Barry was an altruist with a simple but strong
        defensive character plus an enthusiastic and
        sanguine temperament. His popularity and
        leadership was unchallenged.

        Jones was an egotist with a complex and proud
        character combined with a querrelous and
        bilious temperament. His life-long frustration
        which kept him a bachelor can be traced to his
        failure to woo and wed Dorothea Dandridge
        who became the wife of Patrick Henry, the
        great American orator and governor of Vir-
        ginia. Owing to the fact that Jones had killed
        a man in his early life at sea, he changed his
        name from John Paul to John Paul Jones in
        order to create a new identity. The stigma of
        the escape of the "Glasgow" wrongly placed
        upon Jones the charges of incompetence. Jones
        was a supreme naval fighter but proud in the
        conceit of his leadership.

7th: Sea Service:
        Merchant Marine: Barry from 1760 to 1775—
                                      15 years
                          Jones from 1760 to 1775—
                                      15 years
        American Navy: Barry from 1775 to 1803—
                                      43 years
                          Jones from 1775 to 1788—
                                      13 years
        Russian Navy: Jones from 1788 to 1789—
                                      2 years

8th: Land Service:
        Barry assisted General Washington in the cross-
        ing of the Delaware River and also in the Battles
        of Trenton and Princeton.

9th: First War Prize Captured by Barry on April 7th,
        1776—British Sloop "Edward".

10th: Priority of Naval Commission:
        Barry was "Captain" on "Lexington" Decem-
        ber 7th, 1775.

Jones was "1st Lieutenant" on "Alfred" December 7th, 1775.

Jones became "Captain" on August 8th, 1776 on the "Providence".

11th: Barry received Commission No. 1 in the new American Navy on June 14th, 1794 from President Washington. The following is the exact letter from Secretary of War, Henry Knox:

War Department, June 5, 1794

Sir: The President of the United States by and with the advice and consent of the Senate has appointed you to be a Captain of one of the ships to be provided in pursuance of the act to provide a naval armament herein enclosed.

It is to be understood that the relative rank of the Captains is to be in the following order:

John Barry
Samuel Nicholson
Silas Talbot
Joshua Barney
Richard Dale
Thomas Truxtun

You will please inform me as soon as convenient whether you accept or decline the appointment.

I am, sir, etc.

HENRY KNOX
Secretary of War

CAPTAIN BARRY

In using the title "Commodore" to John Barry's name, the reader should remember that this title was used freely by the Navy Department, especially with the ending of Barry's sea-service, the official communication addressed to him on June 11th, 1801 was written thus:

Navy Department, June 11th, 1801

Commodore Barry, Philadelphia:

The law providing for the peace establishment of the Navy, a copy of which I now enclose, directs the President to select from the Captains 9 gentlemen, from the Lieutenants 36, and from the midshipmen 150, to be retained in service. The duty is unpleasant where gentlemen are not retained. On the present occasion it is particularly pleasing to me to have the gratification of informing you that the President has been pleased to select you as one of those who are retained."

It must be noted that Barry had served with honor, both Washington and Adams during their presidencies, and this letter came from the new Secretary of the Navy under the newly elected President Thomas Jefferson who had broken the power of the Federalists and ordered severe retrenchments which included the stoppage of building new vessels and reduced the entire U.S. Navy to thirteen vessels. At the time of Jefferson's inauguration, Barry's squadron was at sea and he was ordered by Secretary Dearborn to give orders to the squadron under his command to "call home all the ships in the West Indies and make the best of your way to Philadelphia." Barry reported his arrival in the Potomac on May 23rd, 1801 and received the above communication on June 11th, 1901 from the Secretary of the Navy with the salutation of "Commodore Barry."

12th: Sea-Battles:
There is little doubt that all the biographers of Jones have made the major event of his life the Sea-Battle between the "Bonhomme Richard" and the "Serapis" which took place off Flamborough Head on September 23rd, 1779. The skill of battle shows Jones with a defective ship not engaged in outmanouevering and utilizing its gun-fire against another ship which had the potential of sailing ability and gun-fire which it

could not use, but the battle shows the "Bon-homme Richard" as an old hulk in a death-grip with the "Serapis" which did not require the seamanship and fighting skill of two disen-tangled ships engaged in range warfare. How-ever, it must be granted that this battle re-quired exceptional courage and doggedness in clinging to the "Serapis" plus much deck fight-ing in hand to hand combat. Credit must be given to Jones for his personal bravery and victory. If you have read his own words con-cerning the battle, you will understand better how his victory was accomplished. (Page 55 Chapter VI).

The raids of Barry were many and his capture of the British Sloop "Edward" on April 7th, 1776 was the first prize of war. The words of Barry himself were always few and routine, however his engagements in sea-battles as of May 28th, 1781 of the "Alliance" with the "Atalanta" and the "Trepassy" and on March 10th, 1783 of the "Alliance" with the "Sybille" as well as his capture of the post war French vessels engaged in raiding American maritime commerce, these manifestations of courage, seamanship and naval tactics in normal battle array speak for themselves.

13th: Achievements:
Barry led the "Compellers" in forcing the sign-ing of the Constitution by Congress.

Barry fought for equal pensions to soldiers and sailors.

Barry became leader in civic affairs of Phila-delphia.

Jones negotiated for the settlement of war prizes in Europe.

Jones received from King Louis XVI the honored title of "Chevalier" and the "Cross of the Order of Military Merit."

Jones served for one month as American Con-sul to Algeria.

14th: Honors and Memorials:
From his lonely lodging rooms, Street of Tournon, No. 42, Paris, Jones received a military funeral from the French Government but the location of his embalmed body was forgotten and apparently lost for 113 years. It was found by Ambassador Porter and brought to America in 1905 by Admiral Sigsbee, U.S.N. In the year 1906 the body of Jones was interred in the sarchophagus of the Memorial Tomb beneath the American Naval Academy Chapel of Annapolis, Maryland.

The original sculptored bust of Jones by the French Sculptor Jean Antoine Houdon has been copied many times and many oil paintings which are found throughout the world are held as memorials of his historic personality.

Because of his pronounced association with Free Masonry, Jones has been honored in many ways throughout the world.

"Barry Day" was established and observed in the States of Massachusetts and Pennsylvania. Herewith is the official Proclamation designating September 13th as "COMMODORE JOHN BARRY DAY" by His Excellency Edward Martin, Governor of Pennsylvania.

PROCLAMATION

In the Name and by Authority of the

COMMONWEALTH OF PENNSYLVANIA

Governor's Office

Harrisburg, Pa.

COMMODORE JOHN BARRY DAY—SEPTEMBER 13, 1944

Since the earliest days of the American Republic the Commonwealth of Pennsylvania has had a large share in the growth and expansion of the United States Navy. Today, the naval forces under the Stars and Stripes are the most powerful the world has ever known.

As our fighting ships and planes strike crushing blows at the strongholds of tyranny it is appropriate that we honor Commodore *John Barry, Father of the American Navy*, who gave distinguished and heroic service at sea in our Nation's struggle for independence. His brilliant exploits have placed him foremost among the heroes whose skill and daring have brought everlasting glory to the Navy of the United States.

After the Revolution, Barry turned his talents to the establishment of the American Navy. His efforts were rewarded in 1798 when the Navy Department was created by Congress.

Therefore, I, Edward Martin, Governor of the Commonwealth of Pennsylvania, in accordance with the letter and spirit of the Act of August 5, 1941, P.L.810, do hereby proclaim September 13, 1944, the anniversary of his death in Philadelphia, September 13, 1803, as Commodore John Barry Day. I recommend that the day be observed by our people, and in the schools to perpetuate the memory of this great American patriot.

> GIVEN under my hand and the Great Seal of the State, at the City of Harrisburg, this eighteenth day of August, in the year of our Lord one thousand nine hundred forty-four, and of the Commonwealth the one hundred sixty-ninth.

(Signed)

EDWARD MARTIN

BY THE GOVERNOR:

(Signed)   *Charles M. Morrifon*
Secretary of the Commonwealth

Barry was buried with military honors in old St. Mary's Cemetery Philadelphia, and a Requiem Mass for the spiritual repose of his soul was celebrated in St. Mary's Church.

The following Epitaph was engraved upon the vaulted marble tomb of Barry. It was composed by Dr. Benjamin Rush, M.D., eminent American, Protestant, Signer of the Declaration of Independence and life-long friend of the Barry Family.

LET THE PATRIOT, THE SOLDIER AND THE CHRISTIAN
WHO VISITS THESE MANSIONS OF THE DEAD
VIEW THIS MONUMENT WITH RESPECT.
BENEATH IT ARE INTERRED THE REMAINS OF

JOHN BARRY

HE WAS BORN IN THE COUNTY OF WEXFORD IN IRELAND
BUT AMERICA WAS THE OBJECT OF HIS PATRIOTISM
AND THE THEATRE OF HIS USEFULNESS.
IN THE REVOLUTIONARY WAR WHICH ESTABLISHED THE
INDEPENDENCE OF THE UNITED STATES HE
BORE AN EARLY AND AN ACTIVE PART AS A CAPTAIN IN THEIR
NAVY AND AFTER BECAME ITS COMMANDER-IN-CHIEF.

HE FOUGHT OFTEN AND ONCE BLED IN THE CAUSE OF FREEDOM.
HIS HABITS OF WAR DID NOT LESSEN HIS
VIRTUES AS A MAN NOR HIS PIETY AS A CHRISTIAN.
HE WAS GENTLE, KIND AND JUST IN PRIVATE LIFE,
WAS NOT LESS BELOVED BY HIS FAMILY AND FRIENDS THAN BY
HIS GRATEFUL COUNTRY.

THE NUMBER AND OBJECTS OF HIS CHARITIES WILL BE
KNOWN ONLY AT THAT TIME WHEN HIS DUST
SHALL BE REANIMATED AND WHEN HE WHO SEES IN SECRET
SHALL REWARD OPENLY.

IN THE FULL BELIEF IN THE DOCTRINES OF THE GOSPEL
HE PEACEFULLY RESIGNED HIS SOUL INTO THE ARMS OF HIS
REDEEMER
ON THE 13TH OF SEPTEMBER, 1803, IN THE 59TH YEAR OF HIS AGE.

HIS AFFECTIONATE WIDOW HATH CAUSED THIS MARBLE TO BE
ERECTED TO PERPETUATE HIS NAME AFTER THE HEARTS OF HIS
FELLOW-CITIZENS HAVE CEASED TO BE
THE LIVING RECORD OF HIS PUBLIC AND PRIVATE VIRTUES.

These words are inspirational for every American and together with the bronze plaques on the Fourth Street front of Saint Mary's Church, they become monumental and historical. Monuments which dominantly proclaim the importance of Commodore Barry can be found throughout the United States but best known of all are those in Washington, D.C., and Philadelphia, Pennsylvania.

In the Centennial Year of 1876, the Catholic Total Abstinence Union of America erected in Fairmount Park, Philadelphia, at the foot of George's Hill a large fountain with one of the five statues of heroic size as that of Commodore John Barry. The Friendly Sons of Saint Patrick donated on March 16th, 1907 to the City of Philadelphia the bronze statue which surmounts the granite pedestal on the commons of Independence Hall as well as the beautiful oil painting of Barry by the famous artist Gilbert Stuart which hangs within the historic walls of Independence Hall of Philadelphia. In Washington, D.C., Congress passed a bill signed in 1906 by President Theodore Roosevelt for the erection of the Barry Monument in the nation's capitol. Of great importance was the launching of the U. S. Torpedo Boat Destroyer "Barry" in the Philadelphia shipyards on March 22nd, 1902 and its christening by Miss Charlotte Adams Barnes, daughter of Captain John S. Barnes, U.S.N. of New York, and also a great-grand-niece of Commodore Barry. The oil painting placed in Independence Hall since March 18th, 1895 was declared by General St. Clair Mulholland to be the living image "of the Father of the Navy of the United States—the Navy that from the beginning has become the admiration and model of all the nations of the earth". The oil painting which hangs upon the walls of the White House was painted by Gilbert Charles Stuart, the American artist whose portrait of Washington is considered the best ever painted. This masterpiece was quite eloquently shown to the millions who witnessed the television itinerary of the Presidential Mansion by none other than Mrs. Jacqueline Kennedy who referred to it as the portrait of Barry—"Father of the American Navy."

Commodore Barry Monument, Independence Hall, Philadelphia, Pa.

EPILOGUE
For God and America!

In these atomic days of the "Space Age", we cannot help but remind our readers of the substantial and truthful participation of Commodore Barry and other Catholics in the discovery, development and defense of the United States of America. From the three Catholic discoverers of America, namely, Brendan in 550, Leif Errickson in 1000 and Columbus in 1492, down to the Catholics of Revolutionary days, we shall find thousands of others serving both God and America. We acknowledge the fact that there were many non-catholics who believed in General Washington and fought and died for the cause of Independence! We also declare that these self-same patriots emulated the spirit of President Washington by living in peace and harmony with our forefathers and always gave due credit to the following Catholic leaders who belonged to the same tribe of God's chosen people to which Barry belonged. We feel that it is our duty to leave this memorial of patriotism and service to the reader who may better understand our Faith and Loyalty for God and America!

Colonel Stephen Moylan—Head of the Commissary Department and Colonel of the Light Horse Dragoons.

General Count Casimir Pulaski—Father of the American Cavalry.

General Thaddeus Kosciusko—Father of the American Artillery and author of a Textbook for Cadets on "Artillery Manoeuvers." He was also the builder of the first Military Academy at West Point and became a national champion of liberty for Negroes.

Brigadier General Louis L. Portail—Father of the Engineer Corps and first topographer and engineer of Valley Forge Encampment.

Colonel John Fitzgerald—Aide-de-Camp to General Washington.

General DeLaRouerie—Valiant officer who fought with Washington and afterwards returned to France and died as a martyr for his faith.

General Jean Baptiste Rochambeau—Assisted in the capture of British forces and surrender of Lord Cornwallis st Yorktown.

Chevalier DeLuzerne—Diplomat who financially aided the American Revolution and after whom Luzerne County in Pennsylvania was named.

George Meade—Financier to the starving troops at Valley Forge.

Don Juan De Miralez—Legate from Spain and Friend of the Colonies.

Thomas Fitzsimmons—Pennsylvania's Signer of the Constitution.

Daniel Carrol—Maryland's Signer of the Constitution.

Thomas Lloyd—First Official Stenographer of Congress.

James Lynch—First Marshal of Continental Congress.

Charles Carroll of Carrollton—Signer of the Declaration of Independence.

Rev. Ferdinand Farmer, S.J.—Missionary, Philosopher, Scientist and Trustee of the University of Pennsylvania.

His Excellency, Archbishop John Carroll—First Catholic Bishop of the United States of America, who accompanied Benjamin Franklin on a diplomatic mission to Canada.

It is your privilege of liberty to select your own friends but it is your prerogative as a rational being to be just and honest in your decision as to who was the "Father of the United States Navy". The author of this monograph on the basis of "greater service for American Independence," gives to Commodore Barry the accolade of honor of being "Father of the United States Navy." With humility the author admits that this book deals with cold facts and he leaves the task of further research to the reader with the hope that the heroic records of "Barry or Jones" will become the instrumental means of inspiring all Americans to know, love and serve God and America!

Bibliography

Letters and Manuscripts—John Paul Jones—John Henry Sherburne
Life of John Paul Jones—James Otis
John Paul Jones—A Sailor's Biography—Samuel Eliot Morison, U.S.N.
Life of John Paul Jones—John S. C. Abott
John Paul Jones—Man of Action—Phillips Russell
Origin of the Flag—Prebles
Watson's Annals of Philadelphia and Pennsylvania—John F. Watson
                                                Willis P. Hazard

Catholics and the American Revolution—Martin I. J. Griffin
Commodore John Barry—Father of American Navy—Martin I. J. Griffin
The First Captain—Story of John Paul Jones—Gerald W. Johnson
Life and Times of John Paul Jones—Mrs. Reginald De Koven
Paul Jones—Founder of American Navy—Augustus C. Buell
John Paul Jones in Russia—Dr. F. A. Golder
History of Philadelphia—Scharf & Westcott
Administration of the Revolutionary Army—Hatch
Records of American Catholic Historical Society
American Catholic Historical Society Researches
Catholic Historical Review
Life and Times of John Carroll—Peter M. Guilday
History of Society of Jesus in North America—Hughes
History of Roman Catholic Church in U.S.A.—O'Gorman
American Catholics in War—Williams
Irish Contribution to American Independence—Maginnis
Pioneer German Catholics in the United States—Schrott
Leopoldine Foundation and the Church in U.S.A.—Roemer
Woodstock Letters
Memoirs of Rev. Augustine Bally S. J.—Schuyler
Old Jesuit Trails in Penn's Forest—Fink
Little Journeys around Old Philadelphia—Barton
Sketch Book of Pennsylvania—Bowen
George Washington and Town of Reading—Nolan
From Quebec to New Orleans—Schlarman
Catholics and Declaration of Independence—Lenhart
Catholics in Colonial Days—Phelan

Life and Times of Archbishop Carroll—Shea
Manuscripts and Lectures—Clare Fenerty
Manuscripts and Monographs—Mathew Carey
Addresses—Cardinal Gibbons
Lectures—Archbishop Ireland
Captain John Barry—*Portfolio July 1813*—Dennie
Biographical Dictionary—*1809*—Allen
Naval Biography—Frost
Sages and Heroes of the Revolution—Judson
Catholic Church and German Americans—Colman J. Barry, O.S.B.
Mullen Memorial Library—Catholic University of Washington
The Library of Congress—Washington
Collections of American Catholic Historical Society
St. Charles Borromeo Seminary Library

Acknowledgments

Acknowledgment with gratitude for research courtesies.

Mullen Memorial Library—Catholic University of Washington

The Library of Congress—Washington

American Catholic Historical Society of Philadelphia

Library of St. Charles Boromeo, Overbrook

The ATHENAEUM of Philadelphia

Philadelphia Maritime Museum

Mr. William V. Elder, Registrar, The White House, Washington, D.C.

Miss Marian Fenerty

Norman J. Griffin, Esq.

Index

(135)

Other Books by the Same Author

PAUL—Hero and Saint

PETER—Commander in Chief

JOHN—Apostle of Peace

DOCTOR LUKE—Beloved Physician

FATHER STOMMEL—Church Builder

OLD JESUIT TRAILS IN PENN'S FOREST

GOOD SHEPHERDS OF IRELAND

TRILOGY OF THE HOLY NAME

PRILGRIM TALES—Poems of the Holy Grail

THE VERGILIAN EULOGY

MOVING MOUNTAINS

JUST ORDAINED

GRADUATE NURSES

MEMOIRS OF
GENERAL HARRY CLAY TREXLER

FROM BALLY TO VALLEY FORGE

UNDER THE SILVER MAPLE

BUCKINGHAM PALISADES OF THE DELAWARE

MONSIGNOR HEINEN

THE FESTIVAL OF TARA

THE SACRED OAK OF THOR

THE BLACK ROBE OF HURONIA

CATHOLIC INFLUENCES UPON THE LIFE OF
FLORENCE NIGHTINGALE

BERKSHIRE SHEPHERDS AND THEIR FLOCKS